Praise For 52 Things...

Essential reading for those who want to cut through all the hype of big data. This book has practical advice on how to have real financial and business impact, from the experienced authors who have done this in real life.

John Forsyth
Former Principal (Partner), McKinsey, former Head,
McKinsey's Global Customer Insights Practice

•••

Significance. Reliability. Confidence. These and other such terms can be a mantra for both suppliers and buyers of data and analytics. Whether it be big data, qualitative research or something in between; sampling, statistics and "findings" are often the drivers of customer or business analytic exercises. But what about relevance? If the results cannot direct business decisions, what does it matter how "accurate" they are? Used correctly, such analytics are an enormously powerful driver of business performance and profitability. But only if the findings have business salience or business significance. Otherwise, aren't they just another type of BS?

In this book, Mike and Alex Sherman lay out some wonderful examples of how the time and money spent on business analytics can transform decision-making or be a complete waste of time. It contains great lessons for buyers and users of such services. But I would also commend it to consultants and suppliers. We shouldn't need to sell what a computer can do with data. We should be promoting what humans and businesses can do by asking the right questions of the results.

Adrian Chedore
Former CEO of Synovate

•••

It is easy to pay smart people a lot of money to do clever analysis that too frequently still leads to dodgy decisions. Much better to use Mike and Alex's hard-won, real-world experience so you can avoid painful pitfalls, ask better questions, and get the insights that matter to your business. Great job!

Matthew Willsher
telco CEO/CMO with over two decades of experience in
Australia, Hong Kong, Korea, Malaysia, Nigeria, UAE and the UK

***

Mike is a great leader, industry expert and orator in his field.

Mike and Alex have written a book not just for analytics professionals but for everyone. The book raises and clears critical questions plaguing the industry.

A book written for data scientists by a truly talented and highly experienced individual who lives, eats and breathes analytics! A must read!

Abeed Rhemtulla
Managing Director and Founder, Enigma Group, sponsor of Analytics
Leaders Conferences across Asia-Pacific

•••

Mike and Alex have delivered an entertaining and highly readable romp through many aspects of customer analysis—from qualitative focus groups through to terrabytes of big data; and utilizing many real-world examples to reinforce their points.

They employ a relentless focus on the use of analysis to deliver meaningful and impactful business value ... and that should matter to you, too, whether you're the CEO, the product owner or a junior analyst delivering the work.

George Haylett
Former Asia Analytics Head for Amex, Citibank and HSBC

•••

Data analysis is only valuable when it leads to decisions. I saw this mantra in action when Alex worked with us, helping us develop and deploy online strategies that attributed to a significant increase in traffic to our website, as well as bolstering sales. Alex has created a book that uses relatable stories with practical advice to achieve business impact from customer analytics.

Brian Linton
Founder and CEO at United By Blue

•••

This book provides invaluable guidance for realizing business value from consumer insight analytics efforts. The authors insightfully explain the practical and strategic aspects of analyzing consumers and their data by using many well-chosen stories and examples that are thematically organized. Mike and Alex show us that even with -- and especially with -- the ever increasing power of the methods and tools for automating consumer insight analytics, real business value will only be realized if the managers and consumer insight data scientists involved in the analytics work clearly understand the important questions, how these questions relate to what data is useful, and how that data should be (or should not be) used. In short, this book thoughtfully and practically reminds us that as we continue to further automate consumer insight analytics efforts with the newest analytics and AI technology, human thinking and human understanding of the fundamental purpose of the analysis and of the questions that are essential to that understanding that purpose becomes even more important.

Professor Steven Miller
Vice Provost (Research), Singapore Management University

52 THINGS

WE WISH SOMEONE HAD TOLD US

ABOUT

CUSTOMER

ANALYTICS

By ALEX SHERMAN and MIKE SHERMAN

Copyright

Title: 52 Things We Wish Someone Had Told Us About Customer Analytics
by Alex Sherman and Mike Sherman

Classification: Non-Fiction
ISBN: 9781726601061
Imprint: Independently published

Cover design by Panagiotis Lampridis, The Design Lab
Cover Illustrations:
Who is Danny/Shutterstock.com
Peshkova/Shutterstock.com

Preface

Welcome.

Books on customer analytics (data science, business analysis, market research, whatever you like to call it) primarily exist in two categories: as academic texts, which discuss theoretical approaches to data analysis problems; or as technical texts, which teach the statistics or computer programming required to conduct an analysis. As the focus of these books is on analysis tools and techniques, fictitious examples are often used to explain main topics.

What's missing are real-life, practical stories, tying analysis directly to business value. That is the objective of this book.

This book is for anyone who uses customer information to make business decisions: CMOs, CEOs, marketing directors, product owners, consultants, and the people who provide that information: data scientists, market researchers, business analysts, statisticians, subject matter experts. By tying impact to tools and techniques, through real-life stories, we hope to help decision makers better understand how to practically use customer data while helping data analysis providers to better understand how to create output that end users will value.

Enjoy.

Introduction

Ours should be the golden age of customer insight.

Many, if not most, companies cite the importance and priority of being customer driven, customer focused and customer friendly.

> *"We see our customers as invited guests to a party, and we are the hosts. It's our job every day to make every important aspect of the customer experience a little bit better."*
>
> **Jeff Bezos**
> Founder & CEO of Amazon

•••

> *"Your website isn't the center of your universe. Your Facebook page isn't the center of your universe. Your mobile app isn't the center of your universe. The customer is the center of your universe."*
>
> **Bruce Ernst**
> VP of Product Management at Monetate

•••

> *"To succeed in business today, it's essential to capture the hearts and minds of your audience quickly, before your competition does. To do that, you must put your customers first, in everything you do."*
>
> **Denyse Drummond-Dunn**
> Former Global Head and VP Consumer Excellence, Nestle

•••

> *"There is only one valid definition of business purpose: to create a customer."*
>
> **Peter Drucker**

At the same time, the ability to win based on physical product differences is diminishing.

> *"Products are no longer competing against each other; they are collapsing into each other in the minds of anyone who consumes them."*
>
> **Youngmee Moon**
> HBS Professor and Author of Different: Escaping the Competitive Herd

•••

There are also more sources of customer data than ever before—big data tracks our behaviors in myriad ways, while social media provides a pathway for us to naturally share our thoughts, feelings, and interests.

Yet, despite all of this, customer analytics[1] is not viewed as a senior partner by business leaders. In survey after survey, CEOs, CMOs, and others cite the relative ineffectiveness of research and analytics in bringing the voice of the customer into business decisions.

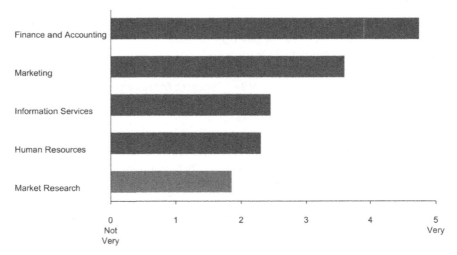

CEOs Get Limited Value From Market Research
How useful is the information?

"It should pay to know more about our customers, but too often we get a huge data dump without the kind of insight that will drive results."
CEO of a financial services company,
quoted in BCG's The Consumer's Voice –
Can Your Company Hear It? November 2009 (p. 6)

•••

1. In this book we use the term customer analytics; please view it as encompassing similar terms such as market research, customer insight, customer analysis, data science or business intelligence. We believe all cover the same topic, that is understanding customer behavior: what people do and why they do it.

Introduction

Asked whether, generally speaking, she is happy with the quality, Marjolein VanNieuwkasteele, Chief of Global Marketing Management at Philips Electronics, answers with a blunt: "No." …

Many researchers are still uncomfortable with providing clear, concise recommendations."
Research World, April 2005 (pp. 13–14)

•••

We believe that the contents of this book can help bridge that gap between opportunity and reality.

Some of our insights are based on Mike's over 30 years of experience as a research and big data user at Procter & Gamble, McKinsey, SingTel, and Hong Kong Telecom and a research provider at Synovate (now Ipsos).

Notably, Mike's observations are not based on one market or one industry. He has visited or worked in more than 125 countries, held several regional and global roles, and been based in New York and Hong Kong. He has also touched almost every major industry including consumer goods, retail, telecoms, financial services, technology, and covered consumer, SME, and B2B categories.

Alex brings a deep understanding of new economy tools and techniques with his own experiences leading natural language processing projects at an analytics vendor (SAS) and a leading global technology firm. He has taught hundreds of students how to apply machine learning to practical business problems as a data science instructor at General Assembly. Additionally, Alex has lived, worked, and studied across the globe in the United States, South Africa, Hong Kong, and Singapore.

In many ways, this book is a collection of our conversations over the last few years. Accordingly, while the book blends our separate stories together, we wrote it as a single narrator to keep the focus on the business value of each story. Some of the stories are Mike's, some are Alex's, but we have chosen to use the editorial "we" for all but a few stories.

The book is organized around six sections:

Section One

Emphasizes the importance of connecting any work to business impact, otherwise we're just wasting our time

Section Two

Talks to the importance of choosing the right evaluation metric, so that the output connects to the business metric (usually profit)

Section Three

Discusses how to collect data to get what you need and avoid wasting time with useless data

Section Four

Focuses on understanding data to avoid common traps that lead to misuse or misunderstandings of the data

Section Five

Focuses on various tools and techniques, and how to analyze the data to create insightful, practical output

Section Six

Concludes with suggestions for clearly and concisely communicating output, as a good output that is poorly understood is unlikely to achieve much impact

The book is written in short chapters to be picked up and read one chapter at a time, in whatever order suits you. Each chapter focuses on one or two ideas, which we introduce with a clear "so-what" statement, followed by the necessary theory, and then real, practical examples of these ideas in use.

As we hope to help our readers bring the voice of the customer into their work, we would like to do the same. We welcome your thoughts, feedback, and ideas. You can reach us at Mike@MikeSherman.net and AlexShermanCustomerAnalytics@gmail.com as well as see more of our work at www.MikeSherman.net

Contents

Section Four
UNDERSTANDING DATA: ALL DATA IS EQUAL, BUT SOME DATA IS MORE EQUAL THAN OTHERS
69

Section Five
USING DATA: THE DRILLS AND THE HOLES
104

SECTION ONE

DRIVE FOR IMPACT: SHOW ME THE MONEY!

Our first set of stories revolves around the importance of connecting any work with a positive business outcome. At for-profit businesses, the metric is easy: profits or return on investment. The metric for not-for-profits or governments can be more difficult but the point still applies—make sure that your output helps the client achieve their ultimate objective.

To illustrate this critical lesson, we share stories built around the following:

- Inspirational quotes from Ted Levitt (Chapter 1) and Jerry Maguire (Chapter 2)
- A framework for selecting how to decide what projects to take on (Chapter 3)
- The four levers to create profits (Chapter 4)
- Advice on how to deal with difficult clients (Chapter 5)

1
Show Me The Hole!

Focus on the outcome, not the tool.

One of our favorite quotes is:

> "People don't want to buy a quarter-inch drill. They want a quarter-inch hole!"
>
> Ted Levitt
> Harvard Business School

In both traditional market research and big customer data, the practitioners love to wax lyrical about their "drills": how big they are, how fast they go, how sophisticated they are, and so on. But all too often they lose sight of the purpose of the drill—to create the "hole".

Instead, let us realign that focus toward things that help managers make better business and marketing decisions. Some may wake up in the morning wishing for more research or more data, which is dreaming about the drill. This often leads to wasted time and effort. Rather, in your sleep, we hope you have thoughts about the decision makers who need guidance and wake up realizing you can provide some missing information or insight to help them make those decisions; that is dreaming about the hole.

Big data is rife with an unproductive focus on tools. There is the data itself, from myriad new sources, and the hardware and software to process it. Necessary (sometimes) but not sufficient. To this point, during one project, we heard a client complain about a meeting with an analytics software vendor. He grumbled, "Technologists too often speak about the features of tools based on how long the feature took to create or how interesting they find the technology, not how much value they provide!" If you are focusing on the tool and not the hole then senior decision makers are not interested.

A friend and former colleague shared a problem over coffee. She was advising a university and one problem they had was predicting students who were unlikely to graduate in the typical four-year period, or often, at all. The belief was that those who exceeded four years often did not finish, and so the university sought to identify those "at risk" and take appropriate action. Our friend was working with a statistics professor and they had looked at all sorts of data (commute time, method of commuting, if the student had a child, etc.) using various modeling techniques, hoping big data would identify at-risk students. But their output was not very predictive.

Our suggestion was that they go a simpler route. Graduation required 120 credits or 15 credits per term. They should look for students with fewer than 60 credits after two years. If students were less than halfway done after two years, likely they wouldn't finish on time. Not perfect, but probably a good indicator and very actionable!

FRINGE BENEFITS

When output is easy to understand, it is more likely to trigger practical solutions. In the example above, our colleague was reminded of a related problem relevant to students who likely would not graduate in time. Students were identified as full time if they took 12 credits in a term, but graduation in four years required 15 credits per term. Therefore, there were some students who might be surprised to learn they would not graduate on time. (Let's hope they were not the math majors.)

Applying big data tools and techniques wasn't helpful in this case; focusing on the problem using traditional analytic and research techniques was far better at identifying and helping address the problem.

Because most of our anecdotes and lessons focus on the hole, that does not mean we ignore the drill, just that we see it for what it is: a tool, a means to an end, not the end itself. Sometimes you really need to understand the drill to be able to create the right hole. (Do not try drilling into cement without a masonry drill.) Ultimately, it should always come down to how to use the tool to create the end product, not to confuse the two.

2
Saint Jerry Maguire

Spend your energy on the results that matter.

Why is Jerry Maguire our patron saint of customer analytics? Because of the seminal line in the movie, delivered by Jerry (Tom Cruise) at the repeated urging of his client Rod Tidwell (Cuba Gooding, Jr.), "Show me the money!"

We often begin training sessions by asking why people do research or data analysis. The answers usually begin with statements about understanding customers, testing new products, understanding competitors' products, establishing market share and so on. Then, when we keep pushing, eventually (we hope) someone says, "To make money." It is this link between the guiding business objective of making money and the specific research task that is often forgotten.

This is a critical imperative that needs to be taken seriously by marketers, analysts, insight providers, researchers and others. If we cannot link our work to revenues and profits, then why should management care? Too much research is defensive, undertaken because "We needed some numbers to justify the decision we had already made," or "Maybe we'll learn something useful." For management to pay attention, we must repeat the mantra "Show me the money!"

The concept works in reverse as well. Show someone the money and the cost of obtaining that insight becomes less of a barrier. We learned this lesson early when we were at a meeting negotiating a new project. The client said something to the effect of "This is a very expensive project." Chuck Farr, the senior McKinsey partner responded that the impact of the project would be in the hundreds of millions of dollars, while the cost was in the hundreds of thousands (this was a long time ago). He said he wanted to work with people who focused on capturing the big opportunities, not worrying about the relatively small cost of doing so. We got the project.

We experienced this upon joining Synovate. We were assisting their Business Consulting division with a proposal that the client researcher wanted to do but was fearful selling internally given the high cost (about a million dollars). We asked the researcher to estimate the potential impact of the project, which was creating products for the underserved SME division. The response: "If we get this right, we can increase sales 500 million to a billion dollars a year." We made the point that sales of that magnitude surely justified a project costing "only" a million dollars.

Remembering Jerry Maguire and focusing on showing the money helps get the right types of projects sold.

3
Reduce Uncertainty That Matters

Answer the hard questions that count and punt on the easy or irrelevant ones.

We like a quote from Marissa Mayer, former CEO of Yahoo:

> *The interesting thing about being CEO that's really striking is that you have very few decisions that you need to make, and you need to make them absolutely perfectly … you can delegate a lot of the decisions, but there are a few decisions, and sometimes it's not obvious, that you need to really watch and that can really influence the outcome.*

She wants to focus on big decisions that matter, where her guidance is necessary, rather than decisions that either aren't critical or in which her guidance is not essential.

Research and data analytics do not tell managers what to do; they provide guidance. To make that guidance matter, focus on where there is uncertainty that matters.

A simple framework suggests where research and analytics is needed. On one axis is *uncertainty*, from low to high. On the other axis is *value* (or value at risk), again, from low to high.

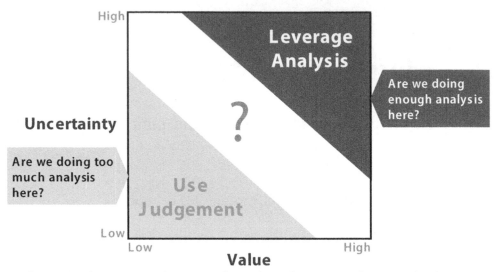

Unfortunately, too much research and analytics are done in the bottom-left corner, where the uncertainty is low (I know what I am going to do, regardless of what the output says), and value is also low (if I get it wrong, it is easy to fix or it won't matter). This is the zone of wasted work: no matter what the findings, it won't change the business outcome, so why bother? Just do what you want to do.

The sweet spot is the top-right corner, where the manager is genuinely unsure of what to do and it matters because there is money to be made or lost. This is what we mean by "uncertainty that matters." Here, research and analytics are welcomed.

Years ago, we were advising a Philippine company on a new project where the CEO was genuinely unsure if he should proceed. This was a new segment for the company and they were unsure if their product would sell. They would have to commit tens of millions of dollars to the project with little recourse if the product did not sell. This, clearly, was a top-right corner issue.

The research brief required results in eight weeks. The response from two agencies: "We need 20 to 26 weeks to do this right—this is a difficult challenge!" The response from a third agency: "You're crazy, you cannot do it that fast here! You want to research affluent people and they are hard to schedule." Our reply to this agency: "We have nine weeks until the CEO has to make a go/no go decision. Results before then are in the top-right corner, results after that are in the bottom-left corner as the decision will have been irreversibly made. So, don't go for perfection—deliver what you can to reduce the uncertainty."

Useful input into the decision was achieved by focusing on what could be done in the relevant time frame. The output suggested customers would buy this new product, but with some substantial changes versus the original plan. The result: a happy CEO who launched the project and was able to show his shareholders the money.

Thank you, Jerry Maguire!

4
How Do We Show The Money?

To "show the money" you need to understand the four levers that increase profits:

1. capture share from competitors
2. capture surplus from consumers
3. grow the size of the market
4. reduce costs without reducing value

If your work is not leading to improvement in one or more of these four levers, it is very difficult to demonstrate how your work will improve profits. Without this link to profits, it is hard to truly engage senior management, for they are always thinking about improving profits.

In Economics 101 we learned about supply-and-demand curves and that industry revenues are the result of the intersection of the two, the area inside the dotted line.

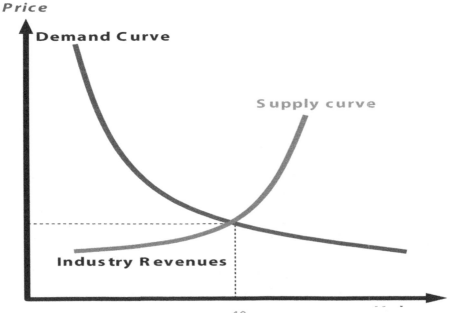

As shown in the chart, to increase revenues and profits, we can do one of four things:

Four Ways To Create Value

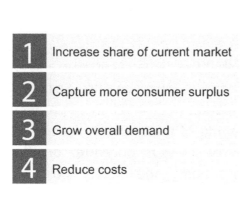
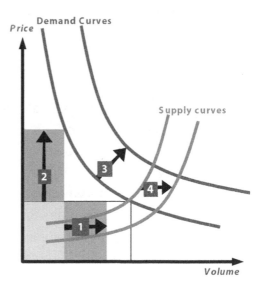

1	Increase share of current market
2	Capture more consumer surplus
3	Grow overall demand
4	Reduce costs

1. Grow share

This is the standard profit-growth scenario. We take revenues from existing competitors, leaving the industry revenues unchanged while our sales grow. This is the classic Coke versus Pepsi scenario with each brand trying to grow by beating the other. A subtler way of growing share is to segment the market to improve the attractiveness of your products. So, with soda, this means shifting from the original cola to diet cola, lemon cola, caffeine-free cola, caffeine-free diet lemon cola, etc. By segmenting the market, the company seeks to shift share towards its brands (and maybe increase industry sales if they cannibalize non-soda sales by people shifting from tea or coffee to diet soda).

2. Grow surplus

When we charge a higher price to some consumers we increase profits by growing margins. This extra value is called surplus. A common example of this model is airline pricing. The same economy seat will have many different prices depending on when the seat was bought and whether the passenger receives small incremental benefits: frequent flyer miles, an extra checked bag, preferred seating and so on. The incremental cost of those benefits is still only a small portion of the increase in ticket price, allowing the airlines to capture most of the price increase as profits, e.g. they capture the surplus.

3. Grow the market

When we grow the total market size, we shift the demand curve up and to the right because we are increasing demand at any given price. So in the chart, we see that due to growth in the market size, we sell more product at a higher average price. A good example of this is the athletic shoe market. Years ago, kids owned one pair of sneakers, priced reasonably. Now, people own multiple pairs (one for running, one for soccer, one for fashion, etc.) and pay more for each than a generic sneaker. So, Nike and others have grown profits by enlarging both the number of items sold and the price per item.

4. Reduce costs

When we reduce costs, we shift the supply curve down and to the right. This has the effect of increasing the volume sold at each price, growing profits because at each price we profitably sell more product. This is not often marketing's domain, but rather product development, where cheaper formulations may deliver the same benefit without affecting customers' perceptions of the product's performance. But it can be relevant in understanding which product features can be removed or reduced without reducing revenue. A good example of this is in the technology area, e.g. mobile phone or PC configuration. Manufacturers create high priced, full featured products while simultaneously offering lower priced, de-featured products. Their challenge is to cut features (and cost) so that they don't cannibalize sales of the high-priced models, while still maintaining attractive margins on the lower priced models.

•••

Growing share dynamically

Growing share means your competitor is losing share; this is the essence of the first source of value. A common mistake is to evaluate initiatives as if the competitor won't respond. But they usually do. So when considering share-growth scenarios, it is better to think dynamically—what will competitors do, how will you respond, how will they respond and so on. Often, a dynamic view will help you avoid bad decisions.

Work we did at a U.S. telco client provides a good example. Their competitor was priced about 5 percent below them and gaining share. The client wanted to stem the share losses and was considering narrowing or fully closing the price gap. However, modeling indicated this would be a poor tactic and the client would be better off competing on quality, hard as that was. Why? Because if the client closed the price gap, they would attract many of the competitor's customers. In the short term the client would win. But when we ran the economics, the losses to the competitor were so great that it was rational for the competitor to drop prices a further 5 percent, restoring the existing gap. If the client again closed the gap, the rational action, despite declining margins, was again to restore the gap. And so it would go until both companies were much worse off. Viewed statically, closing the gap made sense, but viewed dynamically, it would only lead to a ruinous price war.

This same lack of dynamic planning infects the loyalty card business. Loyalty programs for airlines make sense, as the reward is mostly costless: seats that otherwise would be empty. But that is not the case in retail, where the rebates offered cost real money. We've seen several situations where one grocer in a market launches a program and initially sees share gains as customers switch to their store to get the points. But what usually happens is their competitor now feels forced to launch their own program, which wins back the same lost customers. The result, share settles back to the pre-program level but now all competitors have to shoulder the cost of a loyalty program, so smaller, not higher profits. Jerry wouldn't be happy.

The same applies to capturing surplus. It is great when you can add small, low-cost differentiators to a product and raise the price. But it is likely your competitors will notice and introduce a similar product at a lower (but still high margin) price. Play this scenario out and often all the surplus gets competed away in a price war, leaving the market with a higher cost base but no additional revenues.

One example might be movie theaters, as theaters now often compete by offering more and more luxurious seating. When first offered, these seats commanded a premium ticket price, capturing surplus. However, we wonder as more and more theaters match this level of comfort, will the price premium erode, leaving theaters with higher costs yet little price premium?

Increasing Demand

There is an excellent Harvard case study about the introduction of Xbox into Korea. Or the attempted introduction. Growing a category or introducing a new category means that either you will bring new users into the category or increase consumption per user. Otherwise it is a share or surplus gain, not a category gain. Consequently, anyone attempting to grow the category should be focusing on these two sources of growth.

For Xbox, it was about bringing users into the category—game console penetration in Korea was very low. They thought the potential was there because of the existence of thousands of "PC bangs," where mostly boys in their teens and twenties played computer games.

What they should have focused on was understanding latent demand, that is, who did not own a console but would have good reason to do so. Instead, as discussed in the case study, their research focused on existing gamers and especially hard-core gamers, who were asked questions like what kind of games they wanted.

What Xbox failed to understand was that the PC bang was a place to get away from home, not an inconvenient place to play games, and while Mom and Dad encouraged computer use for educational purposes, they were not going to condone gaming (another reason for the kids to play away from home). Moreover, because Korean homes are small, the PC was stationed in the living room not in the kids' bedrooms, as in the U.S., so Mom and Dad could easily see what the kids were doing.

Growing or creating a category means looking for new benefits or solving old problems. Or as Clay Christensen, a Harvard Business School professor, puts it so well: "Understand what job the consumer is hiring the product to do."[2] Perhaps Xbox would have done better if they had looked at young women, who abhorred PC bangs, or at parents, who were seeking educational tools (think about young children who cannot yet use a PC but can use a joystick). But they did not, and as a result they had an unsuccessful launch.

Beyond guaranteeing relevance, asking the question about the source of value may change what you do, who you ask, what you ask them, and how you interpret their answers. For example, if the objective is to grow the market via greater category penetration, then you need to make sure that you include non-category users in the research. If the objective is category growth via greater usage per user, then you need to explore changes in usage. Sounds straightforward and it usually is, if you ask the right question and understand how the client plans to make more money.

So, ask the question "How will this research, analysis, or action show us the money?" Find out which of the four levers your client is seeking to use. If the answer is clear, you have useful guidance on what you need to explore.

_____

2.   Source: Finding the Right Job for Your Product (N9-607-028, September 26, 2006 Harvard Business School).

5
Don't Let The Client Off The Hook

If a client doesn't share the ultimate business purpose of a piece of research or their hypotheses, push them to do so—it is critical to shaping good output.

If the answer to "What is the business problem or opportunity you're addressing?" or, "Which source of value do you seek to tap?" is "I do not know," or, "We just want more insight," then push back. Where there is an unclear connection between the output and action, there is research that senior management does not want to listen to.

What if the client doesn't answer the questions, citing confidentiality or other reasons?

First, explain that answering the question is not about your curiosity but about giving the client a better answer to their issues; that their answer will help you design the right analysis that delivers something more useful (to them and to their bosses). Demonstrate how different business objectives might lead to differences in research design or analysis.

Sometimes client research managers demur because they themselves don't understand the business well enough to answer the question or to even engage their internal client in that conversation. In that case, offer to go with them to the internal client and help them have the appropriate conversation. Show them how to be a better researcher.

Sometimes the internal client hasn't thought through their ultimate needs and speaking with them helps clarify their objectives.

Another objection we've often heard is that sharing their hypotheses about the issues will bias our results. It's true, this could happen. The key here is to explain that you have no stake in the hypothesis and will work as hard to disprove it as to prove it, but to do that you need to understand the hypothesis so you can gather the most relevant information.

Ultimately, if they still refuse, we would suggest not doing the work. In the long term, it's better to focus on work that has impact and not become associated with unproductive work.

The same idea applies to project briefs: insist the client be specific about the business and marketing needs or you run the risk of doing poor or unproductive work. We asked researchers in one Synovate office for real examples of poor research briefs so we could use them in a training session.

Here is one real example: "Hello, I am David from 'client.' Now I am planning to have an MRS study of the newly launched XX product. If we get about N=200 sample for the XX customers, how much does it cost?"

Hard to link this to any source of value. And if this sounds meaningless, it's because it was. There was no objective and so it's unlikely it would have had impact.

When we joined Synovate, a team serving a beverage client came to us for help. Synovate had done quite a bit of research for this client, however, they complained about the lack of insight. How could we help the team unearth more insight from the existing work?

We suggested a meeting with the client to understand their issues and to work out how we could show them the money. "No, thank you," said the client's researcher. "Just mine the existing work and give us more insight." We refused. It took a while, but a few cancelled meetings later, we finally had the discussion. "Our issue is how to grow the category," they said. "We do well with out-of-home consumption but the issue is how to grow in-home consumption. Can you help us figure out how to do this?" At last we had something specific and something an end client would value.

We also had a talented team, led by a very good researcher, which was important because we were addressing an issue not specifically covered in the initial research (which is why you should ask the business objective questions before starting, not after). What we uncovered, with some artful work, was that the hypothesis was wrong. The issue was not in-home versus out-of-home consumption, Rather, the team realized the issue was meal versus non-meal consumption. At home, during mealtimes, no beverage was served (see Chapter 21) but for snack times, beverages were consumed. Likewise, for out-of-home scenarios, the beverage was not present at meals in restaurants, but for snacks, it was.

The lesson here is that if you boil the ocean for findings, you may end up with a handful of salt, but if you start with a "show me the money" question, you will likely end up with something of value.

SECTION TWO

EVALUATION:
PICK THE RIGHT—NOT THE EASY—METRIC

Our second set of stories discusses the importance of selecting the right metric for your work. As discussed in Section 1, usually the objective is to increase profits or the return on investment. Here we discuss the need to make sure there is a clear link between that objective and the output of your work—that linkage is achieved by choosing an actionable, relevant metric.

This is easier said than done. All too often, we've seen the wrong metric used, usually based on comfort with the metric. So, our stories here share:

- Why fuzzy metrics can be fine (Chapter 6)
- How some metrics, like statistical significance, can become poor proxies for evaluating an outcome (Chapter 7)
- Examples of metrics that focus on the wrong outcome (Chapter 8)
- How search metrics are overused because they are easy to obtain, unlike purchase or satisfaction measures (Chapter 9)
- The necessity of good controls (Chapter 10)
- That automating analytics requires thoughtful design, as otherwise the effort required to create useful output may be impractical (Chapter 11)

6

Vaguely Right Or Precisely Wrong

Measure what matters, not what is easy to measure.

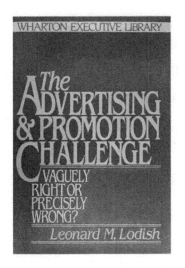

This chapter heading is the subtitle of a great book by Professor Len Lodish of Wharton. He brings this idea to life in his book *The Advertising and Promotion Challenge.*

Like many things, this sounds obvious, but practice shows we do not always do what we know we should.

At P&G in the 1980s, the most common way to test advertising was called day-after recall. We showed a commercial to an audience, either by broadcasting it in a small market or by recruiting people to attend a TV pilot and playing the commercial along with several other real ads within the pilot show. The next day a research agency called people to see if they remembered the advertisement and what about it they recalled. The more they recollected, the better. We also had benchmarks to compare the results with similar brands and categories. So precise!

The problem? Day-after recall does not correlate very well with increases in sales. People remember a commercial but it might not lead them to buy the product. Paradoxically, some others who failed to remember the commercial end up buying more.

There were other potential metrics, but they were "fuzzier," or in Professor Lodish's terminology, "vague." They had less favor, were less conclusive. But as Lodish teaches us, better to use those vaguely right metrics than the precisely wrong ones.

This specific conundrum still exists today. While tools for measuring the impact of a commercial have improved, there is still a lot of reliance on precise, yet potentially misleading, advertising metrics. This is particularly true in the online world, where too often the precise measure of "clicks" is used despite a weak link between clicks and sales.

Dr. Jan Hofmyer, a former colleague at Synovate, took this challenge to heart when he was designing a new brand tracking tool for the company—Brand Value Creator or BVC. He wanted a product that showed the link between brand image and sales. This led him to base BVC on a scale consisting of what brands you bought for your last 10 purchases (and testing advertising by looking at pre/post changes in that answer). Why is this vague? Because the linkage to the advertisement is not clear, and we do not know if people remember the ad, did not like it, were not persuaded, and so on. All we know is whether there is an increase in preference.

Was BVC as precise as day-after recall? Probably not. It seems a bit vague. Was it more useful in assessing brand communications? Absolutely. BVC showed a tighter connection between its measure of brand strength and business performance than almost all traditional brand tracking measures.

The important point here is to search for measures that link to impact, even if there are other, more quantifiable options out there; precision provides comfort, but it may be false comfort.

MAKING BVC MORE PRECISE

One of Jannie's breakthroughs with BVC was to include the impact of barriers that prevent consumers from fulfilling their preferences. For example, "I would like a Pepsi but this restaurant serves only Coke." By including this element in the model, he was able to improve the accuracy between brand preference and the business outcome.

7

Statistical Significance Versus BS

Don't confuse statistical significance with what really matters: business significance.

Statistics 101 taught us what statistical significance means—and we promptly forgot. But we may not realize we forgot, and for many people, they misinterpret what it means.

To remind us all: if something is statistically significantly different at the 95 percent level, it means that if there is a difference between two measures (Brand A is preferred to Brand B) and we repeat the analysis 20 times with different random samples, 19 times out of 20, Brand A will be rated higher than Brand B. What statistical significance addresses is the variability caused by using a sample (assuming we have a normal- or bell-shaped distribution, which is not always the case).

But what it does not tell us is if the difference matters. That is where BS (business significance) comes in. Business significance answers the question: "Does the difference cause you to reach a different business decision?" If it does not, then who cares if it is significant or not? If the purpose of customer analytics is to help managers make better decisions, then what is the value of telling them something that does not aid in that decision?

Statistical significance is still relevant because it reminds us that the difference we base our decision on may be due to randomness, not a real difference. But in our experience, the difference required to reach a different business decision is typically far larger than that required for statistical significance.

With BS in mind, sometimes you can make do with a smaller than desirable sample, and sometimes you get deceived by a large sample.

A good example is found in Chapter 3: Reduce Uncertainty That Matters. In that case, we used a smaller than desired sample. This was required to meet an aggressive timeline. A statistician might quibble with the result, but as noted, some information, even if not fully robust, is better than none when you have a time-sensitive decision to make.

The converse occurred one time when we were in Brazil advising a beverage company and the large sample obscured the business issue. They had tested a new version of the formula for a leading beverage. The results were close to even, something like a 48/52 preference. Even though it was almost even, given the large sample size, the difference was still statistically significant. But there was no BS—essentially, they could choose either formula and customers would be satisfied.

What gave the results business significance was diving deeper to understand regional preferences. The company operated nationally, and due to business constraints, it could use only one formula. Upon digging, it was clear that the lower-scoring formula was strongly preferred in one important market, while the "winning" formula was only weakly preferred elsewhere. Therefore, the recommendation was to go with the less-preferred formula because it likely would provide stronger preference among those that cared, while not being viewed negatively among most others.

A related story from the same work:

With food and beverage products, people will tell you they have strong product preferences, and often they do, but not because of the product. (Likely they are driven by marketing, packaging, availability, and other factors.) Why? Because in many cases consumers cannot tell the difference among products.

While serving the same client in Brazil, a group of us went out to dinner one night. The topic of beer preferences came up, and many loudly proclaimed they strongly preferred Heineken and other foreign lagers to local brands. We thought those who preferred foreign lagers were confidently ignorant, because it is actually quite difficult to differentiate lagers. So, we did a blind taste test over dinner (yes, this makes the results less than clinically pure). But not just tasting Glass A versus Glass B, the standard way. Rather, we had everyone taste Glass A and Glass B. Then we gave them Glass C, and told them it was one of either A or B and asked them to say which. The results: 50-50. Despite a strong belief that the group preferred one brand over another, they could not even tell which was which.

Once the sample is large enough, there is little benefit to increasing its size. At one South Korean client, they had been told that for any research to be valid, it needed to have a sample size of three thousand people. This would get them significance for small differences, but it was overkill considering what was needed for business significance. This became critical because the cost of a piece of research was quite high, partly driven by this large sample size, when a smaller sample of one thousand would have been sufficient at a much lower cost. But the client team was adamant on the larger sample size and ended up funding a too-expensive piece of work.

The opposite can also be true. We once presented findings from a survey of 15 people, and one of the team criticized us, saying 15 people was too small a sample to draw any conclusions. We had to explain that in this case, 15 was appropriate because the total universe was only 16 people (it was the sales force for a commercial product), so the results were, in fact, valid.

What matters is business significance. Don't get distracted by statistical significance; it may lead you astray.

8
The Wrong Metric

Select an evaluation metric that aligns with the business objective. Avoid picking a metric because it is familiar, as doing so can lead you to the wrong solution.

Two questions should define any analysis process:

1. What is the business objective?
2. How do we determine success?

Determining an appropriate answer to the second question is more difficult than it may appear.

To determine the success of an analysis, one must select a metric as the criteria to evaluate how well we answer the business question. However, metrics are often proxies rather than direct measurements of success. What we measure is not the objective; it is just as close as we can get to what matters.

Metrics optimize statistical, not business measures. Thus, we must be careful to understand why a metric was selected, otherwise we may win on the metric, but lose on the objective. When selecting a metric, it is important to focus on the following:

1. What situations it rewards
2. What situations it punishes
3. How much influence each observation deserves

For instance, when building a regression model (e.g. predicting the ideal rental price of a home on Airbnb), we define a curve that we hope generalizes to make predictions in the future. We select a metric to measure

27

(and hopefully minimize) the errors. In the diagram below, imagine each point is a home, the long, sloped line is our model's recommended price, and the errors are the difference between the prediction and the optimal home rental price.

Home Prices and Predictions

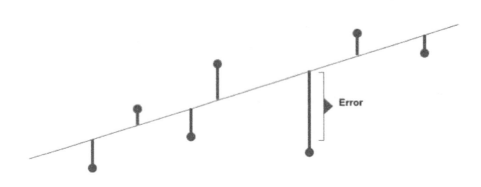

Even in such a simple case, we can create many metrics to measure success. We could move the sloped line to reduce the size of all the errors. This way, our model would provide the best predictions on average. We could move the curve to avoid any error getting too large. This way, our model would avoid providing any outrageous predictions that caused us to price any single home too far above or below market value. Or we could define countless other metrics. There are many options—none of which is perfect—and deciding which metric to use changes the predicted home listing price.

If it doesn't matter that our prediction is off by a little or a lot, we can treat all errors the same. On the other hand, when size matters, we should treat errors differently. Ultimately, this decision—how much we want to punish the error—should be a driving factor in the metric selection.

To explain this point, imagine two rockets landing on a small platform—one on a stationary landing strip, the other on a platform in the ocean. Consider the different punishments for horizontal or vertical error when landing.

For the platform on land, we can treat all horizontal errors the same since if we mistakenly land 10 feet or 100 feet away from the platform, the outcome is the same—we miss the platform and break the rocket! In the ocean, the platforms themselves can be moved to adjust to the landing. Instead of a static outcome (miss and break the rocket), the horizontal errors deserve increasing punishment. The further the rocket strays from the original landing spot, the less likely the mobile ocean platform can be moved to the new location in time (land a few feet to the side and you might be alright, but miss by 100s of feet and fall into the ocean).

On the other hand, the vertical errors are treated the same for both landings—it is hazardous to land too quickly on either platform. Thus, we should increasingly punish the vertical error.

With these considerations in mind, one common error we see is the default selection of a metric because it is familiar, rather than meaningful. Beware of accuracy. It may be one of the most common metrics, but it might not be the right one to use.

We saw this when a client asked us for a model to predict which legal cases met a new federal regulation. Historically, the review process required browsing a 50-page document to evaluate whether the regulation did or did not apply. The decisions were often obvious, but the process was still time consuming, taking 10 minutes or more per document. With 1000s of documents to review annually, the objective was to minimize the time spent reviewing cases, while avoiding mistakes, as there were legal repercussions otherwise. We wanted to automate the process, providing predictions for obvious cases, while limiting any manual human review to only the few, unclear cases.

In the initial request, the client repeatedly asked the question, "How accurately would the model classify the legal cases?" This was the wrong question; accuracy was the wrong metric.

Accuracy is appropriate when you care only about tracking one outcome. When shooting free-throws, accuracy informs the one important outcome: percentage of successful shots. However, in classification tasks we often care about two or more outcomes and need to know the successes and mistakes in each. For the client, focusing on the overall accuracy would have needlessly combined the four possible outcomes:

1. The model **correctly** predicted the regulation applied
2. The model **incorrectly** predicted the regulation applied
3. The model **correctly** predicted the regulation did not apply
4. The model **incorrectly** predicted the regulation did not apply

What the client needed were two entirely different measures:

1. For which predictions are we confident?
2. For which predictions are we not confident?

The objective was to determine which cases to manually review and which to automate. Thus, the consequence for a wrong prediction was drastically different between the confident (trust the model) and unconfident (review the case manually) predictions.

The error for a confident prediction deserved increasing punishment. We needed these predictions to be correct since they would not undergo human review. On the other hand, the error for unclear cases didn't matter at all! These were going to be reviewed manually regardless.

Accuracy did not identify when human intervention was required and when the model was fine on its own. For if the model was 80 percent accurate, we would know that some cases required review, but not which ones. We instead picked a metric that provided a confidence score for each prediction. This allowed us to separate the clear cases (high prediction confidence) from unclear cases (low prediction confidence).

To Review or Not Review: Prediction Confidence

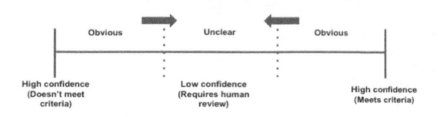

Here is another example we encountered: a model predicting which of five segments a person was in to make sure they received a relevant marketing offer. We had identified five segments and created a relevant offer for each. The offers were ordered so that each segment had a best offer, a next best offer, and then two or three offers that were not relevant. As an evaluation metric, we could have used accuracy to measure how many people we placed into the optimal segment (the first row in the chart below), but that would have been needlessly limiting.

If a person received the second best offer we still could achieve our marketing objective. What we wanted to avoid was sending them an inappropriate offer (e.g. sending a discounted price offer to someone who is price insensitive). This was better accomplished by expanding the definition of accuracy to include the first or second best offer. Further, the business was most interested in segments one, two and four, so we looked at the results for those segments, ignoring the results for segments three and five, which were less profitable. So, instead of measuring overall accuracy, we evaluated the model performance where it mattered (the fourth row in the chart on the next page).

Discriminant Analysis Effectively Identified Segments

	Actual segment					
	1	**2**	**3**	**4**	**5**	*Average*
Correctly identified	64%	58%	45%	41%	44%	**54%**
Related segment	2,3	3	2	5	4	
Related Identification	3	10	22	36	14	14%
Total	**67%**	**68%**	67%	**77%**	58%	68%

We are not offering a complete discussion of statistical metrics; that would take a longer conversation. What we are suggesting is that readers ask the data scientist, or statistician crunching the numbers, what statistical metric they are selecting and how that aligns with the business objective.

9

Interest Is Not Enough

Interest can differ substantially from actions, so beware of placing too much value on search metrics. Instead, try to get access to actual purchase or usage data.

Much is made of all the data that Google and Facebook collect on us. If anything defines big data, it is their data. In Europe, one person used the Data Protection Act to obtain his file from Facebook: it was 1,200 pages long![3] Google and Facebook know all about our demographics, they know what categories we search, what content we are interested in, and much more. But they do not know what we buy or if we are satisfied with these purchases. And that matters.

Nielsen is famous for their reports on grocery store sales, which they also tie in with panel data (purchase data provided by consumers who report their grocery purchases from all the stores where they shop). They report to their clients on a company's category share (actual sales) and use panel data to report on repurchase patterns (a proxy for satisfaction). Google and Facebook cannot do this (yet).

The grocery analogy for Google would involve reporting that you went food shopping, that you entered the aisle where a product is sold, that you picked up and examined a package, but not if you bought the package and not if you liked it. This is critical information if we are to understand our customers.

Contrast that with Amazon's information on books. They know you entered the store (metaphorically), what categories you searched, but they also know if you bought the book and, in some cases, they even

---

3.   Source: http://www.wired.co.uk/article/privacy-versus-facebook

know if you liked it because you wrote a review.

This can make a big difference.

Imagine you browse Harry Potter and the Sorcerer's Stone, the first book in the series. The next time you come to their site, there are three main marketing scenarios:

1. Show you that book again
2. Suggest Harry Potter and the Chamber of Secrets (the second book in the series)
3. Drop it altogether

If you bought the book, certainly do not show it again. If you bought it and reviewed it positively, suggest the second and third books in the series. But if you bought it and then reviewed it as childish fiction or rated it poorly, drop it!

Back to Google. They do not know what you did with the search information. So they often get it wrong. We went to the I-com conference in Spain several years ago, flying from the United States to Barcelona on American Airlines, and then taking a local flight from Barcelona to Seville, where the conference was held. We searched on Google and Travelocity for flights from Barcelona to Seville and bought tickets on the American Airlines and Iberia websites. But Google and Travelocity do not know what we did, just that we searched for flights to and from Barcelona. Now we regularly (still) get ads from a variety of sites, including Travelocity, suggesting deals on flights to Barcelona, long after the need has passed (Barcelona is a very nice place, but we do not expect to be returning soon). They do the best they can with the data they have, but rather than offer a prime opportunity to airlines to market to us, they succeed in aggravating us.

Always aim to get access to actual purchase or usage data. Beware of placing too much value on search metrics since interest can differ substantially from actions.

10
The Good, The Bad, And The Ugly

It is best practice to have a control. One all-too-common example of bad practice is to forgo having one.

Customer Relationship Management (CRM) practitioners know the value of the test-and-learn cycle. They have seen the value of putting a bunch of offers into the market via small cells and then seeing what works. They have seen ideas on a whim succeed and sure-fire ones misfire. They trust in-market testing, which means having a control.

When conducting testing, you need the ability to measure the impact. In most cases, this requires a control: that is, splitting your target group into those getting something, e.g. an offer, a communication, a sales call and a small number of similar people who don't receive anything. Then you track your business metric between the two to determine the impact of the offer. This is good practice and often the only clear way to truly measure impact.

The alternative to a control is to use arbitrary benchmarks, such as the average response rate. But this is hazardous as it can be misleading. Response rates can and do reflect things other than the offer: the time of year, the competitive offers in the market at that time, and other changes in the marketplace. Only a control (ideally a no-activity control, but it can also be a champion/challenger control) allows you to cleanly read the impact. No activity means you don't send anything to the customer, while champion/challenger means you test the offer versus the current best offer (champion).

However, all too often, marketers resist this. They fear that customers will be mad if they don't receive the offer (most don't care, but if you are worried, then send them the offer later, after the test concludes), they fear the impact of lost sales (controls are small, the loss will be minor), or what we often feel is the real reason—they prefer not to have their activities objectively judged. But you must judge: a control helps you measure offer impact, which is necessary if you are to learn and improve over time. It also provides critical data for building response models, which, as we'll discuss later, are the best way to target offers.

This knowledge is also often confounding. Years ago, we were taught the value of controls by the marketers at Readers' Digest, at that time, a leading direct marketer of media content. They tested everything; it was the corporate mantra because every senior manager could regale you with tales of "sure-fire" offers that went down in flames and, conversely, offers tested to humor a junior staff member, that brilliantly succeeded. They trusted the market, measured via a control, over judgement.

Despite this, we've had too many discussions where marketers resist putting a control in place. At one company, this led to our insisting on implementing a control if we were to support any testing, stating, "There is best practice, there is good practice and then there is clear worst practice. Not having a control is the latter and we're not proceeding without one."

A McKinsey story illustrates the value of controls. For candidates from most business schools, McKinsey screens resumes and decides which select few get to interview—there is a limit on how many people they can meet. But at Harvard Business School, they interview everyone who signs up. Why? Because screening does not work, and there is enough potential to justify the effort.

How did they know screening does not work? One year, the recruiting team screened all eight hundred students' resumes, creating a group they would interview and a group they would not. They then put this aside and went about the normal process of interviewing everyone. Then, after the final offers were made, they took out the lists and learned that they would have screened out as many successful candidates as they would have screened in. The screening did not improve the offer yield, it only reduced the total yield. This insight only came about because they took the time to test their judgement and put a control in place.

Recent news articles have discussed how Google is challenging standard HR processes such as interviews and resume screening as, based on analysis of success versus background, these do a poor job in identifying future high-performing employees. Perhaps with all their data, they will develop a better predictor (or have and just don't talk about it).

Implementing a control can be costly, but still worthwhile. Credit card companies routinely let some credit risk happen: they give credit to some people with low credit scores, allowing some potential bad debt transactions to be processed. That way, they have the data against which they can test their model. In this case, the control is not no activity, but activity (the reverse of the normal situations), as the standard protocol is to deny credit to these supposedly higher risk customers.

President Ronald Reagan said "trust, but verify" with regards to ballistic arms reductions treaties. We urge our readers to apply the same maxim to their marketing programs.

11

I'm Sorry, Dave.
I'm Afraid I Can't Do That.

Make sure you have defined a problem that creates useful output.

This is incredibly important with machine learning. Check to make sure you will not create complex output that looks statistically valid but is impractical to use.

Wonkish alert.

Unlike HAL from *2001: A Space Odyssey,* machines are not intelligent enough to know when they have been given a ridiculous task. In consequence, machine learning will do whatever you want it to, except tell you if the output is useful. Therefore, in all data science questions, it is our responsibility to grasp what end users want and define the relevant statistics for the solution. The challenge is translating these responsibilities into a task that is likely to succeed while staying useful for the end user. To meet these criteria, we should answer two questions:

1. Do the conditions for success exist?
2. How much work will success require?

In projects that use time-tested research methodologies, the conditions for success are considered implicitly. We do not question if an analysis of 10 competing products is more laborious than that of two. However, these considerations often get ignored for projects using machine learning, as the difference between a simple and difficult task is not as commonly known.

While the statistics and software engineering of machine learning seem mystical, the underlying mechanics are quite routine. When making predictions without machine learning, programmers write explicit rules into their programs. For instance, to determine if an email is spam, we write rules looking for specific words or phrases (e.g. send money now) to make the classification. Machine learning merely removes the need to create these criteria ourselves. Instead, we let the model extrapolate logical rules by looking at many examples of what happened when these decisions were made in the past. Given the change in how machine learning operates, it is important to question: what conditions would add unhelpful complexity?

To answer this question, we like to focus on three criteria:

1. The number of classes (how many options there are)
2. The frequency of classes (how often each option occurs)
3. The similarity of classes (if the options are easy to separate)

Machine Learning Complexity Matrix

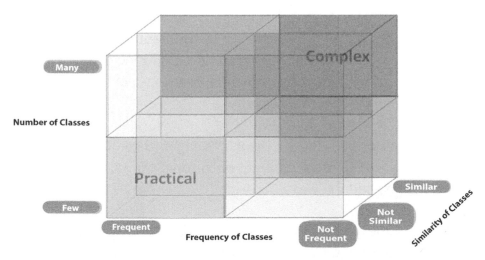

For the first dimension, few classes (Is a restaurant review positive or negative?) are simpler than many classes (What is the restaurant type?). In the second dimension, frequent classes are easier to identify than infrequent classes. For instance, identifying a fraudulent credit card transaction is difficult in part due to the rarity of the event. The third dimension, the similarity of classes, defines the simplicity to separate the classes. Predicting user preference for distinct transportation modes (train or bus) is simpler than similar options for the same mode (Megabus or BoltBus).

One client was concerned about the time staff spent manually reviewing research grants. Dozens of procedures were in place in which a human reviewer read and annotated verbose grant documents. The annotations ranged from funding criteria (Does it apply to funding source A or B?) to research topic (Which of 20 research topics apply?). With recent budget cuts, fewer reviewers were available for an increasing workload, so the client hoped to automate these decisions. Since the reviewers were making their decisions looking at the text of the documents, machine learning seemed feasible. The question was, which of these analyses were worth the effort to automate.

We started with the business objective to predict the funding source and quickly automated the classification. This was a reasonable task: the number of classes was two (source A or B), the frequency was 60/40 so there were lots of cases of both funding sources, and the criteria to apply for each funding source sharply contrasted, so the lack of similarity made it easy to separate the sources.

Delighted with those results, the client was eager to continue and asked us to build a model to predict the research topic. We pushed back; our framework suggested this was a bad idea.

The purpose of the topic analysis was to identify if a grant focused on one of 20 research priorities. Each occurred relatively infrequently; nearly 80 percent of the grants lacked any of the 20 topics. This did not make the problem impossible for machine learning, but it put it in the wrong area of our machine learning complexity matrix. First, there were too many classes to build a reliable classifier with the given time and budget constraints. Second, the topics occurred too infrequently to provide reliable data;

as we noted before, when frequency drastically differs among classes, the problem becomes harder for machine learning techniques to work effectively. Ultimately, we abandoned the analysis.

When a question starts off too complex for practical machine learning, we should try to redefine it to make it simpler. For the research topic analysis, we asked if the output would still be useful if we combined some of the related topics. In that case, it was not an option. But in another example, we did just that.

A student from one of our trainings was working on an analysis of angina, a type of chest pain caused by reduced blood flow to the heart. The analysis began with four types of angina that were difficult to distinguish without extensive medical training. The classes were too similar, so we asked if we could combine the four types of angina into a single objective—any angina type exists or does not exist. In this case, it was appropriate. The output of determining whether any type of angina was present or not was still meaningful. We effectively translated the objective into a simpler problem that still provided useful output.

By keeping the complexity of the problem in mind, you can determine which tasks are worth pursuing and those which are unlikely to provide enough business value to be worth the effort to complete.

SECTION THREE

COLLECTING DATA: YOU CAN'T ALWAYS GET WHAT YOU WANT ...

Our third set of stories discusses the importance of collecting useful data. An old saying still applies in today's world: GIGO— garbage in, garbage out. We've experienced many situations when misunderstanding the data, asking the wrong question, or failing to collect the right data have distorted the output, making it difficult, if not impossible, to deliver actionable, insightful outputs.

Our stories here discuss the following:

- Making sure you don't miss critical questions (Chapter 12)
- Wording questions to get actionable rather than just interesting information (Chapter 13)
- Getting information when people are reluctant to answer the question (Chapter 14)
- Why choosing among alternatives is more helpful than asking what is important (Chapter 15)
- Being aware of cultural bias when wording your questions (Chapter 16)
- The importance of consistency in measuring trends (Chapter 17)
- Fake data that was mistaken for the real thing (Chapter 18)
- Why data privacy is really about giving people value for sharing their data (Chapter 19)

12

Why Didn't You Ask Me That?

Respondents can't answer a question you don't ask: use qualitative research to identify the right questions to ask.

Qualitative research, such as focus groups (six to ten respondents led by a moderator, with the client viewing behind a one-way mirror) and in-depth interviews (also known as IDIs, which are one-on-one interviews with a single respondent) are often invaluable, not because they provide answers (which they do not) but because they provide questions.

By the time you get to a quantitative survey, the questions are set. The respondent has no chance to say to you, "But I don't understand what you're asking," or even worse, "I have something to tell you about what you are asking, but you are not asking me the right question." Use qualitative research to help you find the right questions and words.

One example of this was with focus groups we were conducting shortly after the launch of prepaid cards at one telco (obviously a long time ago). The product was not doing particularly well, and the objective of the focus groups was to understand why. The moderator spent a bit of time explaining prepaid cards—how they worked and so on—but the group was not getting it. Then one participant asked, "Do you mean a stored value card?" Well, yes, that is the same thing. Suddenly the group came alive because the public transit in that city had long used what it called stored value cards. In this case, even though the label "prepaid card" was accurate, the concept was not really understood until we used the right words to describe it (and then to successfully market it).

Qualitative research is also great for uncovering opportunities. Do not ask respondents for solutions to problems, because that is not their role: they will try to help, but really, they do not know. Rather, qualitative research is helpful because it uncovers the problems that need to be solved—ask participants to complain about a product or service and they will outperform.

A technique we learned years ago from our friends at Hase-Schannen Research, a market research company, is called category problem analysis. To identify opportunities, you go through the three-step process diagrammed below.

First, you have a group whine, being careful to capture a list of the problems.

Second, you have the group rate each problem on severity (high to low) and frequency (high to low). You then list the problems in the high/high quadrant.

Third, you have the group consider themes among the high/high group out of which you can come up with a few opportunities.

Category Problem Analysis: Simple Questions, Insightful Output

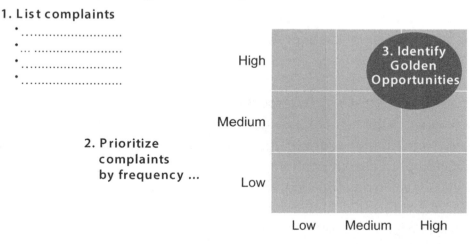

1. List complaints
- ....
- ... .
- ....
- ....

High

Medium

2. Prioritize complaints by frequency ...

Low

3. Identify Golden Opportunities

Low   Medium   High

... and severity

Our favorite example of this—not our own—was when, for a hotel chain, this process identified that a frequent, severe problem was hearing the couple in the next room getting intimate. This led the client to work on providing better room-to-room soundproofing. (We have often wondered if this is what led better hotels to put a mattress between the connecting doors of adjacent rooms.)

Use qualitative research to uncover opportunities or to identify the right way to ask the question—just do not expect respondents to provide solutions.

In most cases.

There were a few times when a group helped the client reach a decision. One was for a European car company that wanted to ship an outdated production line to China, believing they could sell the vehicles to a perceived undiscerning Chinese market. Our team strongly believed this idea was wrong and implementing this would be a disaster, but weren't sure how to convince the client. We did so with a focus group. The client was behind the mirror, the target Chinese customers in the room. The moderator began describing the vehicle, showing some visuals. The reaction of the group was unanimous—they hated the concept. Several of the respondents actually said, "This is a joke, right? When are you going to show us a real vehicle to evaluate?" That was the end of that idea, done in by a focus group.

One other potential benefit of focus groups is to force your clients to really hear what customers are saying. We always insist that the client, even senior clients, attend groups. It is one thing to read about conclusions, it is another to directly confront them. (Videos can also do this but being live is better.) In one situation, we were testing ideas for an integrated PC and TV product. Consumers hated the idea. To them, watching TV was a shared experience, sitting back from the screen in a comfortable den or living room. PCs were ugly things used up-close in a home office or bedroom with unsightly wires hanging from them. They didn't see the two mixing. The product manager was behind the mirror and literally started pounding on the mirror as consumers killed his product, "You idiots, you don't understand why this is a great product!" he yelled. (Fortunately they couldn't hear him.) The "idiots" weren't the consumers, but rather the client who was listening but refused to accept what he was being told. Shortly after, the product was put on hold, indefinitely.

Use qualitative research to identify the right questions to ask. Remember, respondents can't answer a question you don't ask.

KEEP YOUR CLIENTS HIDDEN

When you do your focus groups, a best practice is to have the client present. But make sure they are behind the mirror, not in the focus group room. Why? Because often they misbehave. One time in Japan, a male manager wanted to sit in the room during a focus group for Victoria's Secret (a lingerie company). No way, we insisted, will Japanese women discuss Victoria's Secret products (and usage) with a male present in the room. We almost had to drag the manager out of the room!

13
Ask The Right Question

Stop boiling the ocean and take the time to identify the right questions. Asking a few, exacting questions creates shorter, more enjoyable surveys that respondents engage with, making your analysis easier and clearer.

Surveys are often too long, leading to respondent boredom and likely lack of focus on the questions. This is because we mistake quantity for quality. We challenge anyone to suffer through a grid of 20 brands and 20 attributes and remain engaged. We think that if we ask enough questions, the right ones will be there, yes? Maybe, but maybe (probably) not.

Dr. Jan Hofmyer (mentioned in Chapter 6) was a colleague at Synovate and was particularly engaged with this topic. He worked hard in developing Brand Value Creator (BVC) to shift from 30-minute surveys with several mind-numbing grids (five to ten brands, rated on 20 or more attributes) to focus on the few questions that mattered in evaluating brand equity. He was able to eliminate the need for those tedious grids with just three short questions.

But short questionnaires require the right questions, not just fewer questions. Often questionnaires are long because marketers or researchers put in lots of questions in the hope that one of them is the right one. So, with short questionnaires you need to focus on asking really insightful questions.

An example was the development of a survey to test a new product that had several different sign-up options, including phone number, email address, Facebook login, and Twitter handle. The question the client asked us was: "Which does the consumer prefer?" This was an interesting question but not the right one. The business issue was clear: Would the product succeed if only the company's preferred sign-up method was offered? So, we asked a different question, one that probed if consumers would still sign up for the product if forced to use a particular method. This was insightful because it allowed the client to realize how many customers they would lose if they proceeded as planned. (Answer: they would lose too many customers if they proceeded as planned.)

Asking the right question delivered insight and helped solve a business issue.

It can also be important to ask the question in the right language.

One time, we were supporting research for an English-language publication in Asia. We designed a segmentation study in English, the language of the media and the working language for management. Prior to putting the survey into the field, we asked if we would offer a local-language alternative, which is the standard in multilingual markets where you let respondents complete the survey in the language of their choice. In this case, the client didn't like the idea of adding a local-language option for the survey, saying they already knew their readers preferred English. We questioned if this conclusion was valid and insisted that the survey was offered in both English and the local language. The result: more than 80 percent of the respondents chose to take the survey in the local language (despite a prerequisite of being fluent in English). Respondents read the English media not because they preferred English, but because English was the only option.

Take the time to narrow down your questions to the few that matter and then make sure to ask them in a language that is easy for the respondent to understand.

14

I Won't Answer That—Maybe!

Knowing what information you need does not make it easy to acquire. When data is hard to collect, be creative in how you get it.

With customer analytics, we hope to extract key information from the respondent. Yet, unless questioned in the right way, the customer may be uncooperative in providing their answers. Sometimes this is by choice (it is in their best interest not to share); often, this is due to misunderstanding the questions. In either case, you can ask the same question in different ways, so make sure you are asking in a way in which the respondent is most likely offer the information you want.

We have found three helpful strategies to collect data:

1. Reframe the question
2. Remove barriers to providing data
3. Put yourself in the customer's shoes

When at Synovate, we always asked the account team to include the client's total research spending in account plans so that we could understand how important we were to the client. Sometimes the client would tell us their total research budget, but often they would refuse to do so. In the latter case, we would reframe the question to: "What is our share of your spending?" In many cases, they would comfortably answer this, even though it told us their total spending because we knew our own revenues. But some questions are just more comfortable to answer. And if they would not reveal our share, we would then ask for directional data, for example, "Are we 80 percent, 50 percent, or 10 percent of your spending?" Even if not comfortable with giving a specific figure, they often were willing to provide something directional. For example, one client answered, "Oh no, you're not even 5 percent," which served the purpose of understanding our relative position, even if not a precise number (and was quite insightful to management, since the account team thought their share was closer to one third of all spending).

To this same point, OkCupid, the online dating agency, will often ask what appears to be the same question, reworded in many ways to increase the number of responses. As an example, the below questions were all asked in the past on the online dating site:

1. Would you strongly prefer to go out with someone of your own skin color / racial background?
2. If you were going to have a child would you want the other parent to be of the same ethnicity as you?
3. Not to be racist but which ethnicity do you find to be most attractive?

While all three questions are proxies to determine if someone is open to an interracial relationship, the number of respondents varied drastically between the questions. Nearly seven times more participants answered the first question than the last. This is not surprising, as some questions are uncomfortable to answer. Thus, reframing a question can change who responds, how much data you collect and the response accuracy.

We have occasionally wondered why some surveys ask for your age, others for your year of birth. It is the same question just presented differently. Maybe age is perceived more negatively by some while year of birth might be felt to be less value laden. We don't have the answer here, but the point remains: pay attention to how you word questions as it will impact your responses.

Our second strategy to collecting hard-to-get data involves removing barriers, whatever they may be.

In Chapter Three we shared the example of the Philippine CEO who needed a quick answer. One research agency felt it could not deliver. The concern was we needed to reach affluent people for whom the research incentive of a few dollars was meaningless—the people often scheduled the interview (they had to come to a mall to do the research) and then did not show. How did we make it easy for them to work with us? Instead of setting appointments and waiting for them to arrive, we offered to have a car service pick them up and return them home. The cost was minimal compared with everything else, and while they did not mind cancelling at the last minute or even just not showing up, they acted differently when there was a car service waiting outside their home. With a bit of extra spending we were able to get the information we needed from these valuable customers. Offering childcare at research sites is another approach to help convince young parents to participate in research.

Removing barriers is often key when doing business research. In many cases, the employee whom we are interviewing cannot accept any incentive because it can be seen as a bribe or they are otherwise prohibited from accepting gifts. For business interviews, we offer respondents a report sharing some of our findings, to be sent at the conclusion of the study. Many find this valuable, because they often lack insight into what their peers at other companies experience and this provides that insight to them. We have seen this dramatically improve response rates.

Our third strategy is to place yourself in the customer's shoes.

In Hong Kong's night markets, where bargaining for goods is the norm, most tourists pursue similar negotiation strategies. After the shopkeeper states an exorbitant initial price, the tourist haggles back and forth, inching the price downward to (he or she hopes) an acceptable range. The tourist would love to know an accurate unit price of the product, but rarely finds out by bargaining this way.

Placed in the same situation, we take the view of the seller. Knowing we are unlikely to see the same customer again, our incentive is to start with an outrageous price. Some customers may accept this as the normal price. Others would bargain to feel that they received a great deal. Either way, no single transaction for one product is important enough to provide a "fair" price.

Within this context we start our negotiations differently, immediately asking the price for a bulk sale of 10 of the same item (maybe sharing a story that we are buying gifts for a few friends). With this request, we have gone from a random customer to potentially the biggest sale of the day. What may have ended at HK$40 if bargaining for one unit, quickly becomes HK$200 for 10 units. This provides the desired information (HK$20 is a good unit price), even if we end up purchasing only one.

Knowing what information you need does not make it easy to acquire. Sometimes you must be creative in how you get it.

15
Choice Matters

Don't ask people what is important—ask them to choose.

People are not good at disaggregating their purchase decisions: you know what you like, but not how individual pieces contribute to that preference. In more technical terms, you should use "derived importance" (computing importance from choices) rather than "stated importance" (asking them which attributes are more important) if you want to best predict what product or service a consumer will actually purchase.

If we are designing a hotel with a limited budget we could ask potential customers to consider the importance of each amenity (How important is a pool? A health club? A restaurant?). However, if we want to predict what people will actually buy, then we are better off asking them to choose among hotels with the different options (a health club and pool, but no restaurant; a pool and restaurant, but no health club; or a restaurant and health club, but no pool). The same approach can help a phone company understand which elements of a calling plan are most important, or what features will drive someone to choose one car over another.

The technical term for choice research is "conjoint". Paul Green, a professor at Wharton, was one of the pioneers of this method and an important force in the clear dissemination of its value and how it works. What follows may be an urban legend, as many have heard this story. However, we were unable to verify it. Supposedly, early on, Paul tested conjoint on Wharton students, asking them to indicate which attributes were important in choosing an employer upon graduation—for example, job satisfaction, training opportunities, fringe benefits, or salaries. He also asked them to take a conjoint between different potential employment options.

What did he find from the research? That students' *stated* importance indicated that job satisfaction, training opportunities and the like were most important in choosing a job; while the conjoint, or derived importance figures, indicated that *salary* was the most important attribute.

He then followed up and gathered data on the students' actual job choices upon graduation and how the students rated their employers on the various attributes, in addition to their salaries. What best predicted the job they actually took? You guessed it—salaries.

Even if this particular story is apocryphal, this finding has been confirmed by others, which reinforces the point that what we *say* is important and what we *choose* can be different, and choices are more predictive of actual behavior than preferences.

There is ample literature supporting the value of derived importance and why we are not good at disaggregating our decision criteria. Yet despite that, there is an understandable, if misguided, comfort by clients with asking people directly how important something is.

One way we address this is to have end users take their own surveys, especially when we are using conjoint and want them to become comfortable with the results on a personal level, before they see the research findings. On one memorable occasion, the head of a business unit was taking a survey. The survey included conjoint but also, for comparison, we asked for stated importance. His was a company with a long and strong heritage, but one under attack by a scrappy new entrant that had been gaining share. For stated importance, he listed brand as being very important and rated his own company as far superior to the competition. But when we came to the conjoint, where he had to explicitly choose between his brand, at a price premium, and the competitor, he remarked, "I want to choose our brand, but I am finding it very hard to continue choosing our brand at the higher price." On a personal level he was grappling with the same issue as consumers, even before getting the results. He was understanding why making a choice is more helpful in understanding customer behavior.

An additional, humorous story shows the value of choice research and why appearances can be deceptive. At McKinsey, we often led training programs introducing consultants to the value of conjoint. One time we had six partners take the Game of Life. This was a conjoint where the respondent traded off four attributes: wealth (Bill Gates, CEO, Mother Teresa); cars (Rolls-Royce, Ferrari or Honda); stress (at work, on vacation); and sex (daily, weekly, monthly). Having completed the Game of Life, we computed the importance for the six partners of each attribute and showed them to the group without disclosing which result was from which partner. There were two partners in the group with a high importance ("utility" in conjoint speak) for sex. One was easy to guess: he was single, French, drove a red Ferrari. The other partner no one could figure out. When we disclosed the results, people were so surprised they indicated that the results must be wrong—the second partner was known as a deeply religious, family man, not someone with a strong sex drive. The group gained respect for conjoint as a technique, and had a good laugh when that partner, who was in the room, simply turned to the group and said, "I have six children!"

Conjoint example: The Game Of Life

	Attributes	Choice A		Choice B
Tradeoff 1	Car	Honda		Ferrari
	Wealth	Bill Gates	Or	CEO
	Sex	Monthly		Daily
	Stress	Work		Vacation
Tradeoff 2	Car	Ferrari		Honda
	Wealth	Mother Theresa	Or	Bill Gates
	Sex	Monthly		Weekly
	Stress	Work		Vacation
Tradeoff 3	Car	Honda		Rolls Royce
	Wealth	Mother Theresa	Or	CEO
	Sex	Daily		Monthly
	Stress	Work		Vacation

One experience, where we were able to directly compare stated and derived preferences across people of different nationalities, suggests that we are more different than we think we are.

More than 10 years ago, we did some research on PCs in 10 countries across the Asia-Pacific region. We were exploring brand image across these markets, but also gathered information on product feature importance. Except for the keyboard letters, most PCs are similar across markets. Brands and features differ, but the product lines, within a brand and among brands, are similar. We felt this was a good category for testing to see how different nationalities were when assessing a standard product.

We asked people what features were important (stated importance), and asked them to rate different products and the features of those products. We then calculated the importance of product features (derived importance).

As shown below, when we compared the *stated* importance results across the countries, we observed that there were few differences.

What Consumers Say
Consistent Across The Region...
PC Feature Chart – Stated Importance

○ Top 5 attributes

Attributes Top 2 box	Overall ranking**	Australia	China	Hong Kong	Indonesia	Singapore
Attribute A	①	⑤	③	①	③	③
Attribute B	②	①	①	7	④	①
Attribute C	③	8	④	③	①	⑤
Attribute D	④	②	6	④	⑤	②
Attribute E	⑤	③	②	6	8	7
Attribute F	6	9	8	②	7	8
Attribute G	7	10	7	9	②	④
Attribute H	8	6	⑤	10	11	6
Attribute I	9	③	9	8	9	9
Attribute J	10	7	10	⑤	10	10
Attribute K	11	12	12	10	6	11

*Respondents who strongly and somewhat strongly agreed that the statement is important in evaluating a brand
**Based on average of 5 Asian countries above

However, when we compared the derived importance results, there was much more disparity across the top five attributes.

...But Derived Importance Varies Much More

PC Feature Chart – derived importance

○ Ranking differs by more than 2 places

Derived Importance - Ranked By Utilities	Overall ranking*	Australia	China	Hong Kong	Indonesia	Singapore
Attribute P	1	2	(5)	2	(4)	1
Attribute U	2	1	1	1	(5)	4
Attribute F	3	3	(7)	5	(11)	5
Attribute X	4	(11)	6	(10)	(1)	6
Attribute Q	5	4	(19)	(8)	(8)	(2)
Attribute I	6	5	(10)	(22)	(17)	(3)
Attribute Y	7	(16)	(12)	(3)	7	(10)
Attribute Z	8	(19)	(13)	6	10	7
Attribute T	9	9	(14)	(4)	(13)	11
Attribute N	10	(7)	(2)	(13)	(27)	(14)

**Based on average of 5 Asian countries above

While we are not suggesting we extrapolate this across other categories, we did find it interesting that people claimed less difference in what they said was important than what their choices indicated was actually important.

If you want predictive results, don't ask people what's important, ask them to make a choice.

16

A Meal By Any Other Name

Words matter: we need to make sure to ask well-worded questions and be careful that labels don't unintentionally constrain our thinking.

A survey of out-of-home eating habits, conducted regularly in South Korea, showed an unexpected change a few years ago. The percentage of people reporting eating meals at fast-food restaurant chains surprisingly declined. But sales had not changed. This raised concern. What had caused the change and was this a leading indicator suggesting sales were about to decline?

The study probed out-of-home eating occasions, their frequency for meals and snacks, and the brands used, by occasion. But it missed a key distinction.

Imagine a South Korean woman who has left her office at noon, gone to Burger King or McDonald's, eaten a burger, a Coke and French fries, and then returned to her office. Ask her if she ate at Burger King or McDonald's: yes, she will agree. But ask her if she had a meal there and she'll likely say no.

To South Koreans, a meal includes rice. No rice, no meal. An eating occasion without rice is a snack. Because the questionnaire, unintentionally changed how occasions were mentioned, and referred to lunch as a meal rather than just as lunch, there was a big impact on the responses.

The words we use to label something also matter because they influence how people think. Is it a phone? Is it a camera? Does it matter? Kevin Systrom, CEO and co-founder of Instagram, tells us it does matter, as he applied an effective use of labeling in his insight that led to the creation of Instagram. As cell phones became smartphones, most people viewed new phone capabilities, such as the addition of a camera, as features of the phone. Kevin flipped the perspective. Instead of thinking that now his phone had a camera, he realized that now his camera had a network—an insight that led him to create a company based on the sharing of pictures. It is a simple but undervalued trick to toss your traditional way of thinking and use labels to expose different viewpoints. The phone label constrained people's imagination, while the camera with a network expanded it.

To this point, at a global food company that sells condiments, they do not reference hamburgers and hot dogs, rather they refer to them as "host foods." Their perspective is that the role of the meat is to "host" ketchup and mustard, because those are the products they sell. The label is accurate, but it likely leads them to think differently about the meat than their customers would.

Similarly, we've noticed that management at a fast food chain often refer to the "protein" instead of the beef or chicken or fish. We were not sure if this influenced their thinking, but did wonder if this would block consideration of non-protein options.

For a continued discussion on the importance of wording, and an explanation of why you often hear the phrase "energy exploration" instead of "drilling for oil," we suggest reading *Words That Work* by Frank Luntz.

17

Do Not Forget To Look In The Rearview Mirror As You Drive Forward

If consistent historical comparisons are important, be careful when "improving" the data. Changing how data is collected may prevent accurate comparisons with data from the past.

Peer reviewed research is key for credible findings. Building on prior learnings requires that new and old analyses are comparable, to see if they align. We discussed this topic in a meeting with an organization responsible for collecting and distributing medical research. Fortunately, the precision and accuracy of medical imagery were steadily improving. Unfortunately, this was done in a way that made backward comparison difficult, if not impossible.

Every few years a new medical imagery advancement was released in the industry. More precise cameras enabled higher quality medical scans. However, the camera manufacturers were not concerned with consistency; they just cared to design better, faster, stronger machines without providing the new tools with the ability to replicate old measures. Over time, the measurements in each study were indeed improving, but by continuously adopting new technologies, the industry as a whole had made backward comparison infeasible. By focusing on their tools and not their outcome, researchers had made it infeasible to validate new results. So, when someone asked if an old finding still applied, they could not answer the question.

So how do you address this?

1.   Continue to collect old measures in addition to new ones
2.   Update or map the old data with the new

We used this second approach in work with a hospital to update several archaic enterprise data management systems. To ensure that the removal of old systems and installation of new systems did not impact other business functionality (e.g. prevent patients from receiving the correct medications), we needed to identify all the incoming and outgoing data feeds from each system. During the exercise, one field we collected was named imagery. However, halfway through the project, we realized that this field should be split into two: MRI images and X-ray images. To ensure backward compatibility, we required the entire team to review and update the old data. It took more work, but was worth the effort when we were later asked to conduct follow-up work to update the imaging data management system.

Hence, when backwards compatibility matters, don't forget to look in the rearview mirror as you drive forward.

18
Fake Data

Do not forget to ask if the data is real. Too often, training sets or other made-up data gets mistaken as being real.

When studying at Singapore Management University, we completed a team project. The project required customer data on hotel preferences, so the team sent out a survey. Due to few responses, the professor recommended creating mock data to meet the pressing deadline. While drawing conclusions to create targeted offers from the data, one member vehemently disagreed with one conclusion, stating that it was inconsistent with the data. Of course, we challenged, "The real data or the fake data!"

In this case, it was clear that there was fake data created for the exercise. None of the analysis would reach any actual customers. However, don't assume that a company wouldn't mistakenly draw conclusions from fictitious data as one anecdote from McKinsey exemplifies.

We created a consumer products course at McKinsey to have new consultants work with data in a comfortable environment before they began their first projects. Because the purpose was not deep analysis, but rather to understand common types of data, a fictitious Nielsen data set (e.g. market share, distribution, merchandising, out-of-stock) was created with obvious conclusions. Years later, after the training had been passed along, we received a report in which the output from the fake data was going to be presented to clients as if it were real. The data was being used to illustrate a business point, not just for training purposes, which was clearly inappropriate.

In a more famous example, but not ours, the "beer and diapers" case is often used to portray the value of data mining. As the story goes, when analyzing high-margin items, one retailer identified a strong correlation between beer and diaper sales. These are not items one would expect to see together offhand, but you could justify it as the parent going to the store for diapers and buying beer while there. However, like our training examples, much of the story is actually fabricated. It makes a good point about the potential value of data mining, but the example wasn't real analysis. Rather, it was a hypothesis that was never tested.[4]

On a more serious note, a senior researcher at a South Korean agency related the story of having worked with some of his staff on a presentation to a multinational company on their product potential in that market. The data showed a compelling story, suggesting they should enter the market. However, the next day, at the final presentation, the story had changed and the conclusion was far less clear. Afterward, the senior manager asked the researcher why the conclusion had changed—had he found an error in the data or analysis? Sheepishly, the researcher admitted nothing had changed, but he felt it was unpatriotic to encourage a foreign company to enter Korea, therefore he revised the conclusion. The senior manager went back to the client and explained the situation, sharing the correct data. The client was thankful, but he indicated he was not surprised, because he had previously seen this happen in South Korea, where nationalism is particularly strong.

Of course, sometimes real data can be so messy that it might as well be fake. For one project we collected data from a website that maintains records of current and past federal contracting awards—a notoriously messy data set. Upon examination, many fields were unquestionably inaccurate and others were populated with data from the wrong fields. All in all, we decided to discard the data as it was so untrustworthy that any analysis would be unreliable.

Too often training sets or other made-up data gets mistaken as being real. While it may be fake, the repercussions will be very real.

---

4.   http://www.dssresources.com/newsletters/66.php

19

Data Privacy—Take My Data, Please!

Almost everyone gladly shares their data when they get something of value in return.

Much is written about data privacy, and governments and others are increasingly active in promulgating rules governing data privacy and who can collect, store, and use your data. Much of this is driven by the belief that we do not trust others to have much data about us and we want to be able to limit the ability of others to access that data.

We disagree. We think the real issue is having data used for your benefit, creating a win-win for the marketer and the customer, not stopping people from using your data.

If you ask an audience whether they are concerned about data privacy, many will raise their hands. And if you ask who would like to get less spam, even more will raise their hands. Of course, the only way to deliver less spam is to know enough about you that you are only sent relevant messages, and that requires access to your data. We believe the bigger challenge is not around privacy but centers around delivering less spam and more relevant, welcomed messages, which means using your data for your benefit rather than to harass you.

The point was brought home early on in our work creating McKinsey's CRM (Customer Relationship Management) practice. We presented on CRM to a group of Northern European senior partners. Their reaction was that maybe CRM would work in the United States, where people did not mind sharing data, but it would never catch on in Europe, where people valued their privacy. (Keep in mind this was before Facebook, which proved no one really cares about privacy.)

We challenged them. We asked if their citizens would be willing to share their data if they got something in return. No, they said, they value their privacy too much to share personal data. So we asked if they personally would voluntarily and willingly share their personal data to get some benefits. No, they said, they would never consider it. "Really?", we responded. Then we asked, "How many of you have frequent flyer memberships?" Everyone raised their hands. "But that is different," they said. "We get miles and status and ..." You get the idea. Privacy seems desirable in the abstract, but once you offer something in return, like miles and status, privacy is quickly forgotten.

For us the challenge that is presented as "privacy" is really about one of transparently giving consumers control of their data so they can demand something relevant in return for sharing their data. Give them that choice and they will gladly share.

SECTION FOUR

UNDERSTANDING DATA:
ALL DATA IS EQUAL, BUT SOME
DATA IS MORE EQUAL THAN OTHERS

Our fourth set of stories discusses the critical need to understand your data: what information the respondent was really providing (think about what question they answered, not what question you asked). This applies equally to direct questions (traditional surveys) and to customer data—in both cases, it is too easy to misunderstand the data.

Our stories here share lessons learned that cover:

- The impact of cultural bias (Chapter 20)
- Artificial categorization (Chapter 21)
- Getting underneath the nuances of data specifications (Chapter 22)
- Grappling with different points of entry to an online store (Chapter 23)
- Data veracity: how accurate the data is (Chapter 24)
- Why big data makes your work harder, not easier (Chapter 25)
- Creating new, useful variables from thoughtful reinterpretation of existing data (Chapter 26)
- The value of consulting experts, especially those closest to the problem (Chapter 27)

20
Seeing But Not Understanding

Context matters: our conclusions are influenced by our perspectives, even if we aren't aware of it.

Context is regularly forgotten in research and analysis, especially with international research, where people often forget they are viewing the situation through their own lens. Sometimes our view is complete and correct, sometimes it obscures the truth.

In this image, why is this woman wearing a mask?

Of course, this is a trick question. You cannot answer without knowing the context.

Where is she? If she is in New York or London, she is likely wearing the mask to protect herself from air pollution. If she is in Tokyo, she is likely wearing it to protect others from herself because she has a cold. So, in these two cases the intention is totally opposite; in one case it is to protect herself, in the other it is to protect others.

Otherwise, if she is in India, she might be a Jain, as Jains often wear masks to avoid accidentally inhaling insects and harming them. And if she is in Hong Kong, it probably means that SARS has returned. In other words, there are at least four interpretations for the wearing of the mask.

A similar story comes from Singapore, where, on our second day of work, we went to the ground-floor deli and saw turkey on the menu. Turkey is rarely served in Asia, so we rhetorically asked, "Is it really turkey?" The server replied, "Yes, it is turkey ham." "Wait, is it turkey or ham, because they are different animals and they do not crossbreed." "Look, do you want it or not?" the server angrily responded. We later learned that "ham" in Singlish (Singaporean English) means processed meat; it bears no relation to the British English word that means a pork product. What made this exchange so interesting is that we had no idea there was a different meaning for the word ham and neither did the server. Both of us thought that English had only one meaning for the word ham.

Cultural bias might also lead you to miss the critical question!

A while ago, a grocery chain in China wanted to sell more fresh chicken in its stores. In their market, buying chickens from a grocery store rarely happened because the housewife usually went to the wet market to buy her chickens, which were killed in front of her. Many Westerners would no doubt feel squeamish about the wet market experience in Asia—flies, animal blood, and pungent smells abound. Yet, the Chinese housewife sees the market as the epitome of fresh. The grocery chain's managers wanted to change that perception and hoped their sanitary method of preparing their chilled chicken would triumph over the traditional wet market approach.

They conducted a blind taste test to be used to prove that their chicken was better. But they were surprised. After the chicken was cooked, the housewives could clearly identify which was from the wet market and which was from the grocer.

Of course, this is a marketer's nightmare because in food, anything tasting different from the norm usually means tasting worse. No housewife was going to serve her family "bad-tasting" chicken, no matter what other benefit claims could be made about it.

But that is not the point of this story.

When we shared this anecdote with a group of Americans, they said something to the tune of, "What?! I can't tell the difference between KFC's and Church's chicken. I can't believe they can tell the difference between the source of the meat!"

We, likewise, shared this story with a Chinese colleague. Her reaction was the opposite. She said, "Of course they can tell the difference!"

And then both parties ended with the same comment, "I would not have seen the need to even ask the question."

We are often so clear in our assumptions about human behavior that we fail to ask the appropriate, penetrating questions. We "know" that no one can tell the source of the meat or we "know" they can, so we do not think to question otherwise.

We often find that the solution to this problem is to have a mixed local/ non-local team and encourage each to challenge assumptions and definitions made by the others. It is through this interplay of assumptions that we often uncover the unstated but important biases in how people define both problems and solutions.

21

Coke Is A . . .? What Category Am I In?

Beware of categorizations; they can distort your conclusions!

Categories, such as carbonated soft drinks, are used to help define your competitive set, e.g. Pepsi, Coke, Fanta, Mountain Dew, 7 Up, (but not fruit juice, beer, or water). Volumes within a category are then used to compute market share. But sometimes category definitions blind us to the real competitive set, so make sure your categories truly reflect the consumer's competitive set.

Some categories are clearly artificial and exist for simplified management reporting. We started our career at P&G in the Packaged Soap and Detergent Division, or PS&D. PS&D covered laundry detergent and dishwashing detergent. 70 years ago, the two were the same because clothes and dishes were cleaned with the same product. But since Tide, Dawn, and Cascade were created, that has not been the case. Therefore, everyone knew the management report of share of PS&D was a fictitious category, and any real analysis was done among true competitors. Usually. Except when the share of PS&D declined and it had to be explained. Then, it seemed, people forgot how artificial (and meaningless) that number was.

Several years ago, an analyst's report suggested that the low per-capita sales of Coke and other carbonated soft drinks (CSDs) in China versus other developing countries might be due to lower pricing. That may have been the case, but by thinking about beverages, the analyst may have missed a potentially more important cause—the category definition. [5]

In the West, beverages are the main way that consumers ingest liquids

---

5. China: Not the same Golden Opportunity Across Staples, Morgan Stanley, June 21, 2005, page 15

with their meals and snacks. So, for those markets, comparing the per-capita consumption of beverages and beverage categories like carbonated soft drinks (CSD) could be useful. But beverages are not as commonly consumed during meals in Asia. Quite often, company cafeterias in Korea and China serve a lunch with no beverage—there will be a water cooler with small cups at the exit. The issue is not Coke versus Pepsi or even Coke versus juice or Coke versus water.

So, what else might explain the lower beverage per-capita consumption? What is the right competitive set?

Those familiar with Asian cuisine will know that you might not have a beverage at the cafeteria, but every meal will have soup. Of course, soup is another way to consume a liquid, and if you want to sell more beverages, a key competitor and explanation of beverage consumption differences might be soup, not pricing.

How do you avoid making a potential mistake like this? Two things we find helpful. First, as we noted in the previous chapter, we try to assemble a team that combines locals and non-locals. We find that in the interplay among the team, the cultural factors often surface. This is especially true if the team is curious and continuously asks one another why something is the way it is.

The second thing involves thinking broadly, something Chip and Dan Heath effectively emphasize in their book *Decisive*. To come up with good outcomes you need to consciously broaden your scope of options when you are considering alternatives for a decision.

22

Grrr! Data
Without Meaning Is Mean Data

Understand your data before using it—it might not mean what you think it does.

Due to the increased ease of collecting myriad sources of data, it is important to understand technical limitations. Without understanding how data is collected, you may misinterpret its meaning.

When conducting a CRM analysis for a Canadian bank, we came across a field with customer age. We nearly added the field to our analysis before questioning the meaning behind the data. The CRM system added the customer's age at the date the user first signed up for a bank account, but to save computer storage, the absolute age instead of the birth date was saved. No timestamp was added, so we knew that a customer was 45 years old when they signed up for an account, but not how old they were today with no way to calculate the difference. This left the data meaningless.

A current example is data collected from web analytics tools. Imagine you go to a news website like WashingtonPost.com, scroll on the same page, reading a few articles without clicking any links, and exit after five minutes. How long would Google Analytics measure your time on the web page? Five minutes? No. It would list zero seconds. Why?

Like most web analytics platforms, Google Analytics uses timestamps to calculate how long you were on a web page. This means to calculate how long you were on a web page, it needs you to go to a second page so it can create another timestamp to calculate the time delta from the timestamp created on the first page. Thus, by leaving the website before viewing a second page, the reported amount of time is zero seconds.

Intuitive? No. This is not likely what you think it means or the information you want. Therefore, the danger arises that without understanding how data is collected, you might not realize the data means something completely different than it appears.

MEANINGFUL, MEANINGLESS DATA

Even if you understand the meaning of data, sometimes data is meaningless for your analysis. In a talk on dating and relationship advice at Google, Dan Ariely, behavioral psychologist, asked the audience to think about what information they would want to see when selecting among potential matches on a dating site. Body type, height, age, and other demographics were common answers. Then he asked them to think about if the same information was useful for selecting one's best friends. He concluded of course it is not. The data was meaningless so why is it often provided front and center on dating websites. Likely because the data is so easy to collect. But for meaningful analysis, meaningless data is just a distraction.

Meaningful, Meaningless Data [6]

6.　Source: Dan Ariely: On Dating & Relationships | Talks at Google https://www.youtube.com/watch?v=RS8R2TKrYi0

23

Beware Of People
Sneaking In The Back Door

Retailers need to differentiate between a more controlled physical shopping experience and the less controllable online experience.

In a traditional retail setting it is possible to control the user experience. Stores, with few entrances, can lead customers down a desired footpath to display products in a desired order. Think of the linear paths in IKEA that force customers to view ancillary products, or grocery stores' placement of milk in the back of the store, requiring customers to pass by thousands of other products.

In the digital landscape, it is easy to forget that you cannot control how a user navigates your website. Websites are often built with the expectation that users will follow a natural progression, starting from the homepage. However, in matching users with products, online search engines will use information from an entire site to determine what is most relevant to a user's search query. This often means sending a user to a specific product page, not the homepage. Google, not the CMO, determines the first impression of a new user. This means every web page can be just as important as the next.

This point was emphasized with some work we did for a restaurant selection website in Singapore. We helped a team test different restaurant recommendation engines in order to determine how the website could direct the users to better and more appropriate restaurants. The current approach, like most others, was wisdom of the crowds, that is, the popularity of the restaurant based on website views. The business proposition was that a better recommendation engine would draw more people to the homepage, hence the testing.

During a break, participants were asked to perform an open-ended task: "If you are going to pick a place to eat tonight, what will you do?" Despite having just spent 45 minutes with this new tool, they all did the same thing—they went to Google and typed in their request (for example, Italian, Orchard Road, inexpensive). Google then directed them to appropriate restaurant's websites.

The tested website claimed to be the most popular site for restaurant reviews in Singapore, which it was, based on page views. But those page views came not from the homepage (where the advertising revenue was generated), but from the end pages. Google captured the revenue, not them.

When designing a website, don't assume there is only one path to purchase. Be mindful that people could enter through the side door, back door, or roof.

24

... And Some Data Is Just Crap

Consider the source and quality of data before using it.

Big data is often defined by the three Vs: volume, variety, and velocity. More data, from more sources, faster than ever before. We like the suggestion for a fourth V: veracity. Just because you have data does not make it correct, and unfortunately too often analysts fail to question if their data is accurate!

To improve data quality, we like to ask four questions:

1. Why are values missing in the data?
2. Are we missing variables that are important to the analysis?
3. Can we trust the data?
4. What are the incentives of the data creator?

Missing values are a common occurrence. To fill these gaps, imputation methods often use simple heuristics such as the average. However, this approach is flawed when the data is missing for a specific reason.

In one training session, we use a data set with global alcohol consumption statistics. We ask participants to explore the missing values in the data set until inevitably someone notices only five listed continents, but countries from six. Why? The list of continents uses two-letter acronyms and notates North America as NA. Unfortunately, NA is often used as a symbol for "not applicable." Therefore, when opening the file, every North America listing is automatically converted into a blank value. Correcting these values does not require any advanced method, but it does require a bit of human intuition to ponder why the data was missing.

We also like to think about missing data in the context of variables that provide important context, but are missing altogether.

In a personal project, when looking for a new apartment, we automated a comparison of several thousand apartment listings from Craigslist. When plotting the apartment locations against nearby "places of interest" (grocery stores, gyms, coffee shops), there was a noteworthy ~12 percent premium for listings that had several places of interest within a one-mile radius. Yet, most listings only described the apartments themselves without any description of the surrounding area. Thus, any model without the missing data would not accurately reflect the rationale behind apartment price. We suspect many realtors could improve sales by including this information in their listings.

On a similar note, after selecting a new apartment, we were aggravated when we went to sign up for Internet service on the Comcast website. Taunting us, the final submission button refused to work several times. It wasn't until we switched Internet browsers that we could successfully sign up. We are only guessing, but we wonder if Comcast failed to ask which browsers customers used when they analyzed the cause of complaints and so was unaware of this problem.

You should also consider if the data is trustworthy. Garbage in, garbage out still applies, so sometimes you are better off without using the data at all.

Years ago, in the time before big data, a U.S. client spent a fortune building a database on American households for use in driving their direct marketing. The team confidently told management that this expensive effort would shortly bear fruit, especially the outside data they had integrated into the database. We were skeptical. We questioned the veracity of some of the sources they used.

To bring our concerns to light, we asked the head of the division to ask his team to pull his own file and for him to review it for accuracy. As he viewed his "data," he began to laugh. Asked why, he replied that according to the file, the head of household was his teenage son. It turned out that the data indicated this status because, based on the most recent data (that being a warranty card for a new boom box), the son had checked off "head of household." Now, those of us with teenage children understand that often teenagers do think they are the boss, but that is their perception, not reality. Consequently, just because data has been collected does not mean it is accurate.

We encountered the same thing working on a CRM project for a South Korean telco. As part of our initial data review, we discovered that the telco had nine fields for gender, but with no labels indicating to what they referred. No problem, we assumed, because fields three to nine would likely be blank. Not so—a third of the customers' genders were indicated as fields three to nine and we were never able to figure out why or what this meant.

When questioning the veracity of data, we also find it important to consider the incentives of the data creator.

For the same client we also "discovered" that 60 percent of their customers were farmers. Anyone who knows South Korea knows this is not true. But in this case, we were able to discern the cause of the bad data. The sales reps had to collect certain information to open an account, but they were not interested in bothering the customer or impeding the sale. They just filled out the form for the customer and, since no one ever checked or used the data (until we did), the errors did not surface. For occupation, code one was "agriculture"—the misreporting of farmers was due to the sales reps arbitrarily checking code one on most forms as they were incentivized to sell, not to accurately fill in data. What would be tragic is if we had used it to reach conclusions.

Data Often Incorrect

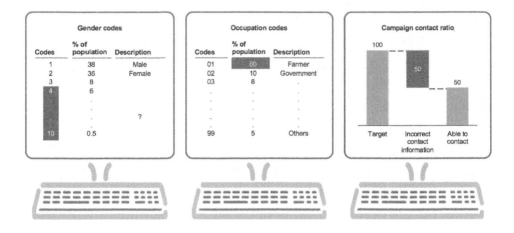

Reviewing data helps to avoid wasting time by determining what data is missing, why it is missing, or if it is so untrustworthy that it might as well be missing.

25
Mo Data, Mo Problems

It is a myth that if you collect enough data, it makes analysis easier; it actually makes it much harder.

Unable to understand their masses of data, clients often ask how to visualize multidimensional data. This is a warning sign. The question assumes that if you use enough data, insight will miraculously emerge. Can adding data help uncover insight? Yes, but not without added complexity. The focus should never be on the amount of data, but rather the relevance of data to a business question.

We consulted with a music and entertainment production company that had made poor choices in selecting a music festival headlining act. To select the headliner—often the most important decision of an event—the client aimlessly amassed data, including online radio trends, social media engagement, search engine activity, and historic ticket sales to name a few. All the data had pointed the client to an obvious choice for a headliner. Unfortunately, the actual ticket sales turned out to be quite meager and the client was hard-pressed to understand why.

We see this approach repeatedly. Clients, overwhelmed by data, lose focus of what information influences the business decision. They concentrate on readily accessible data, eager to act on any salient trend. Yet, without defining what is relevant, attempting to explore all available data obfuscates what matters. The right approach starts with the business objective and then asking what information would help inform the decision (not the other way around!). Often, this does not require big data, just a few key pieces of the right data.

The client's mass of data had identified a headlining act with a captive audience, 10 times that of any other band in the same price category. All the data confirmed this: historic ticket sales were healthy, the band had a large social media audience, and search volume was high and continuing to rise. The data was correct, but was meaningless because, after the failed event, we uncovered that the captive audience lived nearly 3,000 miles from the festival venue—California, not Pennsylvania.

In hindsight, it seems obvious. Why would you hire a band without local fans? But when you have too much data, you can get lost in it. You need to avoid falling into the trap of believing all data has value.

One band that understands this well is Van Halen, as demonstrated in their performance rider. A rider is a band's contract, asserting all performance requirements. On page 40 of Van Halen's lengthy rider, the band famously requested M&M's for backstage snacks, specifying that all brown M&M's be removed. The media took this as superstar extravagance—the egotistical requests of rock stars. However, the actual purpose of the request was to determine if the venue promoter had carefully read and followed the rider in detail.

Van Halen was one of the first bands to use complex pyrotechnics in their concerts. Without a perfect stage set up, dangerous conditions could arise. A lack of brown M&M's meant the band did not need to review the stage setup, but if brown M&M's were there, it signaled that other legitimate safety issues may have been overlooked. David Lee Roth, Van Halen's lead singer, in his autobiography, mentioned that at one venue where the group found brown M&M's, the band's equipment fell through the floor, causing more than $80,000 in damages.[7]

---

7. https://en.wikipedia.org/wiki/Colorado_State_University%E2%80%93Pueblo#In_popular_culture

Van Halen Rider Image

Our highlighting

Twelve (12) fresh lemons (with knife and cutting board)
Cream and sugar

NOTE: Water and coffee must be kept hot continuously with electric hot plates, urns or other suitable devices.

Munchies

Potato chips with assorted dips
Nuts
Pretzels
M & M's (WARNING: ABSOLUTELY NO BROWN ONES)
Twelve (12) Reese's peanut butter cups
Twelve (12) assorted Dannon yogurt (on ice)

Supplies

Forty-eight (48) large, bath-size cloth towels
One hundred (100) cups for cold drinks (16 oz., waxed paper)
Fifty (50) styrofoam cups (minimum 10 oz.) for hot drinks
Plates and bowls (not paper or plastic)
Forks, knives and spoons (metal, not plastic)
Serving utensils, corkscrew, bottle and can openers
Salt and pepper (in shakers)
Tablecloths
Napkins (paper)
Two (2) large bars Ivory soap
One (1) large tube KY Jelly
Three (3) packs Marlboro cigarettes (box)
Ashtrays and matches
Ice (for use in drinks)
Two (2) large garbage cans with plastic liners (for trash)

To determine if the stage setup was credible, the group could have laboriously collected data on each line item in the rider. But checking for brown M&M's was just as indicative. M&M's provided a key piece of information that appropriately answered the business question.

26
Creating Useful Signals From Noise

Big data captures a lot of noise, but sometimes you can transform noise into music! The key is to create variables that focus on solving your problems.

Feature engineering (creating useful variables) is an artisanal process requiring the creative application of domain knowledge. Winners on Kaggle.com, a website that hosts machine learning competitions, often write that their accomplishment was not due to the best algorithm, but rather the most creative use of the data.

Before we speak about the analytics, let's use an example from the real world. Think of the pool table at your local bar—the one that requires a few coins to operate. When hit into a pocket, the only ball that is returned is the cue ball (the solid white ball used to hit the others). But how does the table know which is the cue ball so that it can send it back to the players while keeping the other balls?

Does the table use the size or weight of a ball? No, all pool balls have the same dimensions. Could it be color? The cue ball is entirely white, unlike the other balls with numbers on their surfaces. No, it would be expensive to rig the inside of the table with a camera. Out of guesses?

The answer is the cue ball has an iron core, which a magnet in the table uses to pull it to a separate track leading back to the players.

Cue Ball Iron Core

The iron core in the cue ball was not obvious, but the obvious information was not helpful. We relate to this as decision makers often get caught up in obvious, but useless information. We find that in customer analytics this materializes in the use of demographics, which like the color of a pool ball are obvious, instead of behaviors, which are more useful but like the iron core, difficult to identify. Our challenge in feature engineering is to determine if there is a missing iron core that would help us better answer our business question.

We do not claim to have all the answers regarding how to effectively find the iron core, but we have applied a few feature engineering approaches that have worked well:

1.   Look at behavior more than demographics
2.   Transform the data
3.   Reverse engineer the buying process
4.   Identify decisive moments
5.   Combine similar features

6.   Talk to domain experts (see Chapter 27)
7.   Look for patterns (see Chapter 34)

1. Look at behavior more than demographics
What people do can be more insightful than who they are.

At a Southeast Asian cable television operation, ethnic packages were created and targeted solely based on demographics: Chinese packages for Chinese families, Bahasa packages for Malay families, Tamil content for Indian families, and so on. Although this was safe and avoided selling irrelevant content, it limited the programing sold. By looking for an iron core, we found the language of the content watched.

Extracting the languages watched from the viewing history suggested that some Malay families were already watching Chinese content, and vice versa. The initial reaction of management was that this finding was wrong, so they wanted to disregard it. By the next day, the response changed, "Well, maybe our demographic data is wrong for these families." Or maybe the viewer is in a mixed marriage, or is a child studying Chinese by watching TV, or it is the maid who is watching, or ...? You get the point; it could be for many reasons. As a result, we were allowed to test a model that leveraged this finding and the upsell rates increased substantially. This did not surprise us because if someone already watches some Chinese content, that is a pretty good indicator that he or she might be interested in more, regardless of their ethnicity.

2. Transform the data
Transforming data is useful as it can reveal latent variables.

When teaching, we often write a date and name on a whiteboard and ask how many features we just provided. Most students confidently state: two features! We then explain that from the date we now know if it is a holiday, weekend, period close, and much more. Names come in and out of style, so we can use them to infer age and other demographic information. If you told me your name was Alex, chances are much higher that you were born in the 1990s than the 1960s.

Popularity Of The Name Alex By Year

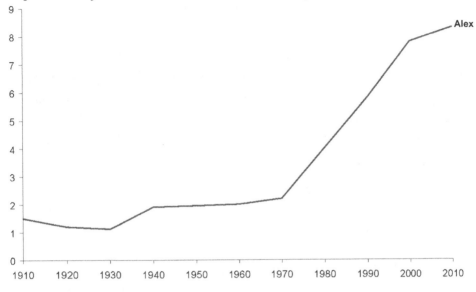

Popularity of the name Alex by year [8]

We have personally seen the value of extracting latent variables like these. For a telecoms client, we had conducted a conjoint analysis which identified five segments, of which two were very price-sensitive. We created a different offer for the customers in each segment, but still needed to figure out who fit into each segment for the majority of customers that were not in the conjoint analysis. To make this determination, we of course would not be able to ask customers the same question as in the conjoint. So our task was to develop a scoring model that used the customer's call records to identify their segment. When we charted the calls by time, we saw lots of "noise" with no discernible pattern among segments. But we had a hypothesis that price-sensitive callers would behave differently.

At that time, calling rates were lower overnight, from 11:00p.m. to 8:00a.m. We created a feature to identify the percent of calls made from 11:00p.m.

8. Google Ngram Viewer https://books.google.com/ngrams/graph?content=Alex&year_start=1900&year_end=2008&corpus=15&smoothing=3&share=&dire ct_url=t1%3B%2CAlex%3B%2Cc0

to 11:15p.m. just after rates went down, and from 7:45a.m. to 7:59a.m., just before rates went up. This derived variable successfully helped to identify price-sensitive callers. As seen below, for the five segments, the most price sensitive made ~10 percent of calls during this 30-minute window, compared with ~6 percent for somewhat price sensitive, and only ~2 percent for non-price sensitive customers. Through a good hypothesis and data mining, we created a useful variable for targeting relevant offers

Telecom Segment Scoring Model: Near Rate Change Variable Helps Predict Price Sensitivity

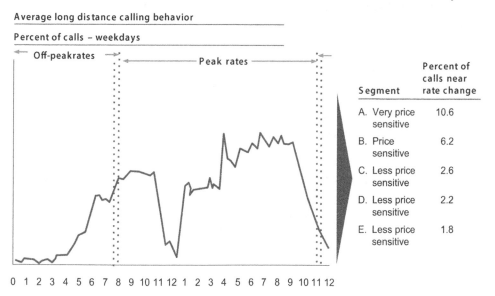

Average long distance calling behavior

Percent of calls – weekdays

Segment	Percent of calls near rate change
A. Very price sensitive	10.6
B. Price sensitive	6.2
C. Less price sensitive	2.6
D. Less price sensitive	2.2
E. Less price sensitive	1.8

0 1 2 3 4 5 6 7 8 9 10 11 12 1 2 3 4 5 6 7 8 9 10 11 12

3. Reverse engineer the buying process

We can also develop useful features by reverse engineering a buying process to identify data that helps predict future sales.

Target, like most retailers, knows that it is difficult to get customers to change their shopping habits once established. However, there are a few crucial moments when a customer is open to change, such as after the birth of a first child. For retailers, this is a profitable opportunity as they may not only capture baby product purchases but also other purchases as established habits change. However, many retailers have access to baby registries, so there is a competitive advantage to identifying pregnant customers before the child is born.

Several years ago, Target had identified a pregnant high school student, sending her coupons for maternity items before her parents knew she was pregnant. The article where this was reported was fear mongering about the mysterious sources of data that companies collect about us, but the prediction was likely from a standard, market basket analysis (an analysis of customer purchases to see which items are often purchased together). By reverse engineering the process, we can think about how they would build a model to identify pregnancy.

Many Target shoppers have loyalty cards, so purchases could be tracked over time. We could use this data to identify new parents by observing who recently started purchasing diapers and other baby items. For these customers, we ask two questions: how did their shopping patterns change nine months ago (at the start of the pregnancy) and how are these patterns unique from other shoppers? It just so happens that during this period, shoppers will start to purchase items such as unscented lotion, hand sanitizers, and washcloths. The single purchase of any of these items is not meaningful, but the repeated purchase of the entire set of items is a potential signal of pregnancy. Of course, no model is perfect. The same items are also used right after someone gets a tattoo, so it would not be surprising if they received the maternity advertisements too.

We have seen the same insight put into action elsewhere by some of our colleagues. A department store wanted to increase sales of camcorders. By digging through retailers' own credit card purchase data, it was apparent that new parents were a key segment as they often bought new camcorders to film their baby. Thus, to target these customers, it was recommended to identify those purchasing maternity clothes to cross-sell them on camcorders with a relevant coupon.

4. Identify decisive moments

We also find it helps to identify decisive moments, those when a timely piece of information can create a memorable experience.

A common challenge for websites is customer acquisition. Mining server logs to attain and retain customers is aimless without a good hypothesis (e.g. Do price sensitive callers behave differently?). One such way to generate useful hypotheses is to identify key moments that matter. Ideally those when a timely (often small) piece of information can change frustration into a positive experience for the customer.

During one engagement, we stumbled upon Enigma.io, a web platform with a public data recommendation engine. After forgetting the password to our trial account, we failed to login after several tries. Avoiding the hassle of what we expected was a multi-step process to change the password, we, instead, left in frustration with no plans to return. Minutes later, we received an email prompting us with a nearly completed password reset form. They made it so simple that we returned to the website. This was not an action that required extensive data mining—it does not take a lot of data to identify that after several unsuccessful login attempts, a user likely forgot their password. Yet, it was a critical moment when a timely email made us product advocates instead of lost customers.

In another case when a timely message mattered, we shifted to Google after a failed search on a different search engine. Seeing we were arriving from a competitor, Google prompted us with a message to consider making Google the default. While there are few times that we would go out of our way to change browser settings, Google identified a decisive moment when there was a clear value proposition to spend the few seconds to update the default search engine.

As a final example of a decisive moment, years ago we were in a terminal waiting to board a United flight from Philadelphia and made a request of the gate agent. While we do not remember the request, we do remember that the agent was not positively disposed to grant it. At that moment, his supervisor came by and he asked him what to do. His response, based on the information on the screen, was to "Give it to him; he pays our salary." We do not know what data the supervisor was looking at, but it was enough to allow him to make a timely decision, and create a good customer experience.

5. Combine similar features

Simplifying your data by combining relevant features helps reveal signals in an otherwise messy data set.

To create informative features, we should ask if our data includes features that we can combine, such as is common in image and file compression. For instance, in the below image we decomposed a picture of a boat into its underlying pixel data. The original image had 720 columns of pixels. We simplified the original image four times, while maintaining an acceptable image fidelity, using a common dimensionality reduction algorithm called principal components analysis (PCA). Even after reducing the original data to only 30 columns (technically, principal components), amazingly, we can still identify the boat.

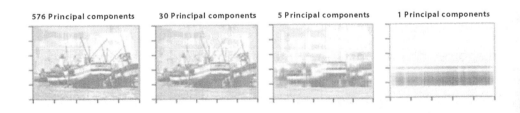

Another case in which there is value in combining data is in working with unstructured text. Informal text is complex as synonyms and misspellings are rampant. Consider terms which have similar meaning, but different spelling (e.g. immediately, immediate, !mmed!ate, instantly). By combining these like-terms, we can create features that contain more signal than when the terms are scattered throughout the data set.

Analyzing text can be complex. One of our students worked as a claims agent for an insurance company and needed to mine text. Every day he would receive nearly one hundred insurance claims. While the severity of these emails drastically differed—some deserved an urgent response, others could wait—there was no way to identify the severity before opening the email. Therefore, the standard process was to respond to emails in the order they arrived.

Recognizing that there was business value in identifying the urgent messages, after the training, the student developed a model to rank and prioritize the claim emails. He accomplished this by training a model to look at the differences in terminology from previous urgent and non-urgent messages. However, it was not until he started to combine similar terms that he was able to achieve near human performance in identifying email severity.

Thus, while we often think of feature engineering as a process of creating new features, sometimes combining or removing data is just as effective.

WHAT MAKES A GOOD FEATURE?

When considering what makes a good feature, we look for five criteria.

Wonkish alert.

Invariant	*When a transformation (e.g. rotation, translation, scaling) is applied, an invariant feature remains unchanged; a covariant feature changes consistently with the transformation*
Stable (Robust)	*Feature should not vary significantly (changes slowly over time; you can keep track of it)*
Unique (Distinctive)	*Individual features can be matched to prior objects of the same type with high accuracy and precision*
Independent	*Values of the variable do not depend on other variables in the model*
Efficient	*Near real-time performance*

To put these into context, consider how companies like Facebook are able to identify and tag users in photos. One early technique was to look at the ratio of facial features. For instance, comparing the ratio from the upper lip to nose, from one eye to another, from the chin to eyebrow, and more. These features are invariant as the ratios stay the same whether the user is near or far in the photo; stable as the ratios do not change much throughout one's life unlike the color of one's shirt or length of their hair; unique as each person has a distinctive set of ratios; independent as they do not depend on other variables like the time of day; efficient as we can calculate these ratios quickly. Models like these help to explain why you are often asked to have a neutral face without a smile for driver's license and passport photos.

For a more mathematical explanation, in the charts below, imagine we are plotting device failure data for cell phones by looking at the deviance of device temperature from the norm. If the red dots represent broken phones and the green dots represent working phones, a model to separate the data in the left chart requires two rules. However, we could use a transformation to create new Y coordinates by squaring the X coordinates to simplify the separation of the data (e.g. 2*2=4). Plotting these values creates the graph on the right. It now takes less effort (just one rule) to separate the classes.

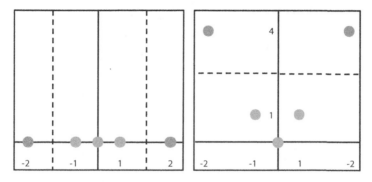

One more example. Consider the same cell phone device failure case in the left chart. It's not even possible to separate the data with simple lines in this case. However, add the absolute value of the X and Y coordinates. For instance, the leftmost point becomes: |-2|+|0|=2. Plotting these overlapping values creates the graph on the right. As promised, it now takes no effort to separate the classes.

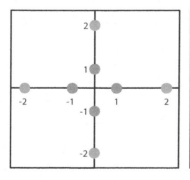
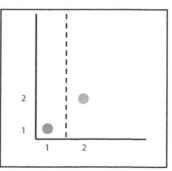

27

Expertise Helps, Often From Unexpected Sources

Sometimes output improves, not with more data, but by talking to someone who brings a different perspective to the analysis.

We rarely find that an analysis is improved by sitting in a room, thinking about what variables to add. Often, getting absorbed in the data shifts the focus away from the business problem. The process should not be what data you can add, but why you would want the data. This implies considering the context of the business question, and talking to end users or thoughtful observers. What you are really looking for is people who look at the business problem differently and will tell you something you are not thinking about.

An example comes from a company that shipped low-value and medium-value items to their customers' homes. To save money, the company allowed for the delivery to be left at the home address even if no one was available to accept the delivery and sign for the items. This led to theft losses, which the company had to absorb. A team was analyzing the theft data and having trouble assessing why certain products had much higher theft losses than others. It was not the neighborhood or other geographic variables, or anything else they had looked at. They were stumped.

Unplanned, someone from the shipping department came by and the team thought they would show the data to him for any insight he would have. He looked at the data and almost immediately said, "I know what is going on! The packages with high theft rates are transparent, you can see what is inside, while most others you can't tell." Problem identified and quickly solved. Not from boiling the ocean, but rather bringing in a different perspective, one that quickly identified the key missing piece of data.

A similar example was from a fast-food chain that was trying to improve their home delivery service by streamlining staffing: they did not want to lose sales for lack of drivers, but having drivers sit around idle was very costly. In this case, instead of getting lost in too much data on the demand for drivers, the team identified one store with a much better driver utilization. They went and interviewed that store manager and learned the key variables to put in the model. The store manager paid attention to which home teams were playing away games that were televised. For those events he made sure he had plenty of drivers, because people stayed glued to their sets and ordered in, but for home games they went to the game, so no need to order in.

Another example comes from combining the world of big data with focus groups. We had developed an actionable segmentation for a European grocer. Using loyalty card information, we combined demographic data from their application (neighborhood, family size) with purchase data from the card. (We had item-level data but for this analysis we focused mostly on total spend and number of categories shopped.) This led to classifying customers as Gold (they do almost all their shopping with us), Silver (most), Bronze (mostly go elsewhere) and Cherry Pickers (only buy deal items).

The marketing challenge was to increase loyalty among the Silvers, who clearly liked us, but also spent substantial sums elsewhere. Analysis of the shopping basket data provided few clues and a lot of confusion. However, after only a few focus groups we had our answer. We told the groups that we classified them as Silver and asked why they didn't do their full shop with us. First, they agreed they were Silver, we had that right. Then they were equally clear on the opportunity: "We go elsewhere because your meat department is awful." They went to a competitor every two weeks or so to stock up on meat, but while there, they did a full shop. With this insight, we were able to confirm it with our data, but we never would have found this pattern by looking only at the data.

We had our answer and the client had a reason to improve the meat department, not just to increase meat sales, but also with the knowledge that this would draw in additional non-meat sales, as silvers would no longer need to do an occasional shop elsewhere.

Sometimes the best insight comes directly from consumers (especially when you can use data to focus on the right consumers) or other experts who work closely with the product.

28

Beware Of Conventional Wisdom

Don't mindlessly accept common definitions or ideas, take the time to challenge if they are true or appropriate for your task.

For one project we were assessing the fast food market for chicken in South Korea. The research had been done: it compared Church's Fried Chicken to KFC, understanding the perception for both with the goal of identifying actions that would help the client build share. At one of the last meetings reviewing the results, someone said, "What about the mom and pop chicken stores?" The client answered that they didn't matter, the battle was between KFC and Church's so the mom and pop stores were not relevant. Caught unaware of this potential competitor, we asked what the person was referring to. He explained that these were small stores, often with a few tables or sometimes just a takeout counter that sold cooked chicken for immediate consumption. It sounded very similar to KFC and Church's purpose. "Are there many of these stores?" we asked. "Yes, over 10,000 spread around the country." At that time, KFC and Church's each had under 100 restaurants. Yikes! At this point the research had been done and we could only acknowledge the gap, but with hindsight we should have collected consumers' perceptions of this format and understood how much of that larger volume could be captured by our client, something we hadn't prepared for.

A similar example, but with a better outcome for the client, occurred in China. This time we were accused of recruiting the wrong participants for some focus groups, but we actually had it right. China's tier four and tier five regions are rural areas and small towns and villages that remain very poor. This research focused on understanding their needs for mobile phones, as the client wanted to introduce a low-cost, low-end product that could penetrate these geographies.

Low-income consumers do have lower ownership of products and services across the board. However, this does not necessarily mean they don't have anything, only that they need to be more judicious in choosing what to buy.

To begin the sessions, the moderator asked the participants to put their phones on the table so we could see what they currently used. Some of those phones were older, second hand, reconditioned phones, which the client assumed would be the case for everyone in these areas. However, others proudly showed off their state-of-the-art Motorola and Nokia phones (yes, this example takes place before the iPhone). The client's immediate reaction was to say that the groups were a waste of time as we obviously had not recruited typical tier four and five customers, whose average annual income was below $1,000 U.S. They "knew" these customers couldn't afford a $300–$500 phone.

They were wrong, the conventional wisdom was wrong, the group was valid. The reality was that some of the phones were gifts from their children: children who had migrated to the major cities but returned home at important holidays like Chinese New Year bearing gifts.

But others had chosen to spend their meager savings on this one important item. While their income was low, their disposable income wasn't as low because they didn't pay for housing and often grew their own food. Importantly, staying connected was a big priority for them so spending this much for a phone didn't seem out of proportion with their priorities. (We should also note that China Mobile, the dominant carrier in China, has excellent coverage even in remote areas. While vacationing in Tibet we told our colleagues they could try to reach us but we'd probably be off network. Nope, even in remote areas of Tibet, we had five bars!)

What was critical to the project was that it wasn't just the ownership that was remarkable, these owners were savvy consumers who could knowledgeably explain product and brand differences. Even if they didn't own a high-end phone, they had seen them and understood them. As such, the plans for the low-end product had to be altered substantially.

In discussing projects, take the time to examine conventional wisdom—it may be correct, but it may lead you to focus on 100 competitors and ignore the 10,000.

SECTION FIVE
USING DATA: THE DRILLS AND THE HOLES

Our fifth set of stories discusses using data, covering both the tools and techniques (from Ted Levitt, the drills), and the output (from Ted again, the holes). For both, we come back to our key message—the tools and the output must be aligned with the ultimate business decision you are helping the client address. Otherwise you get interesting output with little value.

Our stories here share lessons learned that cover:

- How averages can obscure or mislead (Chapter 29)
- The misuse of correlation to imply causality (Chapter 30)
- The case for integrating big data with traditional surveys (Chapter 31)
- The three Ts: why good communications should be Targeted, Tailored and Timely (Chapter 32)
- The case for continued use of traditional, large segmentations (Chapter 33)
- The importance of location patterns (Chapter 34)
- Why response models are useful (Chapter 35)
- How to reduce churn, not just measure it (Chapter 36)
- Media still matters (Chapter 37)
- Why many personalization algorithms fail (Chapter 38)

- Three aspects of pricing
  - » The need to understand perceptions of your price and your competitors (Chapter 39)
  - » How to use anchoring to improve price perception (Chapter 40)
  - » Why real demand curves aren't smooth and how to take advantage of that (Chapter 41)
- How to improve sales productivity by focusing on the best opportunities (Chapter 42)
- Why product performance still matters, but is not sufficient to win (Chapter 43)
- How insight communities—a new research tool—drive better, faster and cheaper output (Chapter 44)

29
The Flaw Of Averages

Averages are often misused; before using an average, consider if it is arithmetically accurate but misleading or misunderstood.

Nate Silver makes this point in his book *The Signal and the Noise*, when he discusses weather forecasting. He points out how forecasters are excoriated when they say there is an 80 percent chance of rain and it does not rain. People interpret 80 percent to mean it will rain, while what it actually means is that for two days out of ten, with that probability, it should not rain. Otherwise the forecast would be 100 percent probability.

Then there are the funny examples many of us learned in statistics class. For example, that the average person does not exist. Of course not, because to be "average" you would need to be half female and half male. There is also the story about the person with his or her head in the oven and feet in the refrigerator who says, "On average, I feel fine!"

But our favorite example of a misuse of averages was from a client who said, "On average, I am a great golfer—my shots go straight down the fairway onto the putting green. But that is a lie because in reality I am an awful golfer—half my shots go left and the other half go right."

On Average I Hit Straight Down The Fairway ...
Half my shots go left and ...

... half go right.

This would all be funny except that sometimes we forget this in the real world. Once, we conducted a conjoint study in China when one attribute was the preference for a laptop or a desktop computer. The analyst, looking at the data, said that attribute was unimportant; the utility (the way conjoint measures importance) of the format attribute was close to zero. But he was wrong: it was not zero for each person, it was zero on average. In fact, people had very strong preferences for one over the other—it was just that half the people preferred a laptop and about the other half preferred a desktop. A very different conclusion. While the average was close to zero, the individual scores were not.

The flaw of averages is another reason why you need to carefully examine your data before proceeding with your analysis. Another time we were looking at average holdings of different financial products. The average for one product was much higher than expected but still within a reasonable range. Was this a problem or an unexpected finding? In this case, it was the former because when we did the histogram of the raw data, we observed one person with holdings of three million dollars, which was the sole factor driving the higher than expected result. In that case, we did go back and look at the original survey, expecting a coding error and that the interviewer had reported $3,000, not $3,000,000. But the interviewer had, in fact, written $3,000,000. This was so unlikely that we disregarded this outlier.

One example resulted in a lot of unnecessary angst. An Asian electronics client was conducting work in the U.S. market to better understand television opportunities. They had data that gave overall brand shares in the market as well as the split among large, medium, and small screen sizes, but in total, not by brand. They were insistent that the groups' participants represented the market, which they specified by brand and size. For example, they wanted one in 25 participants to be a brand C, small-size owner because if you multiplied brand C's share by the share of small size TVs, the result was 4 percent. We had difficulty meeting these (inappropriately, we thought for qualitative research) narrow specifications. In the end, we were unable to find owners of several specific brand-size combinations and the client was quite critical of this recruitment failure.

They should not have been so critical: several weeks later, we had received the detailed brand share information, by size and brand, and it turned out the desired brand did not have any sales in that size in the market where the research was done. By combining the average brand share with the average size share the client had actually specified a null set.

Focus Group Criteria – The Flaw of Averages

Market share, percent

☐ Market data ☐ Interpolation

Brand			Screen size, inches		
			Under 32	32-37	Over 40
			30	40	40
	Samsung	20	20x30=6.0	8.0	6.0
	Sony	15	4.5	6.0	4.5
Brand	Panasonic	14	4.2	5.6	4.2
	Sharp	5	1.5	2.0	1.5 (actually 0)
	LG	6	1.8	2.4	1.8

Imputed share 1.5%, real share was zero, this brand size combination not sold in this market

Data processing (DP) is another source of flawed averages. Any computer can easily create columns of numbers; however, often those columns are filled with numbers that mean nothing (and should therefore be disregarded).

We use a training example taken from research done among pharmaceutical brands in South Korea. We provide the participants with a data table like that shown on page 119. It looks at different pharmaceutical companies and how they are rated: overall, among doctors in hospitals, or in private practices (clinics), among doctors working in different specialties.

Before reporting on the results, we ask the participants to explain what the figures in the various columns mean. They are usually quick to explain what we wrote above, that the ratings reflect the different averages of different groups of doctors. We then press them to explain what the columns for general hospital versus clinic mean. The participants then repeat the definition, usually missing our hint. We then ask if all the doctors answered the same question. We agree they were all asked the same question ("What is your overall rating of this company's drugs?"), but we continue to probe if they answered the same question. To further make the point, we ask if a psychiatrist is answering the same question as a cardiologist. At this point, the issue is clear and someone will say, "No, they are answering the question with reference to different drugs," (or we hope they are because we do not want our cardiologist treating our heart attack with psychiatric drugs!). As noted earlier, context matters.

Armed with this perspective, the participants realize that the combined rating for all doctors practicing in a hospital means … nothing. It is an arithmetic average of answers driven by different groups of drugs. Those ratings are fine within a specialty, where the competitive set is similar, but meaningless across specialties. So the general hospital versus clinic rating reflects the mix of types of doctors practicing in each, not brand strength. The same holds for the columns on the far right, which show geographic results, reflecting that the capital, Seoul, is home to more specialists, while the other regions have more general practitioners and so the difference has little to do with brand strength.

Pharma Brand Strength Data: Many Columns Meaningless

Meaningless average

| | Total | GH | Clinic | GH (General Hospital) | | | CL (Clinic) | | | Area | | | | |
				Cardio-logy	Respira-tory	Psychi-atry	Internal	Pedia-trics	Psychi-atry	Seoul	Pusan	Daegu	Kwangju	Daejeon
Sample Size	500	290	210	58	58	58	110	50	50	240	80	60	60	60
Most Liked Company – Percent	30	33	26	40	43	31	30	28	14	31	35	37	18	27

| | Total | GH | Clinic | GH (General Hospital) | | | CL (Clinic) | | | Area | | | | |
				Cardio-logy	Respira-tory	Psychi-atry	Internal	Pedia-trics	Psychi-atry	Seoul	Pusan	Daegu	Kwangju	Daejeon
Sample Size	500	290	210	58	58	58	110	50	50	240	80	60	60	60
Most Liked Company – Percent	30	33	26	40	43	31	30	28	14	31	35	37	18	27

As Sam Savage tells us in his book *The Flaw of Averages*, beware of misleading averages (except when describing your golf game). Before you start analyzing a data set, consider if the data has meaning. It is easy to create a set of numbers, but just because they show up on your computer screen or among your printouts, does not indicate they mean anything.

30

Correlation Is Not Causality

Statisticians know this but sometimes forget; everyone needs to remember that correlation is not causality.

As shown below, there is a clear correlation between global temperatures and the number of pirates sailing the seas. However, we do not think anyone is recommending increasing the number of pirates as the solution for global warming (at least we hope not).

The misleading correlation of global average temperature with the number of pirates

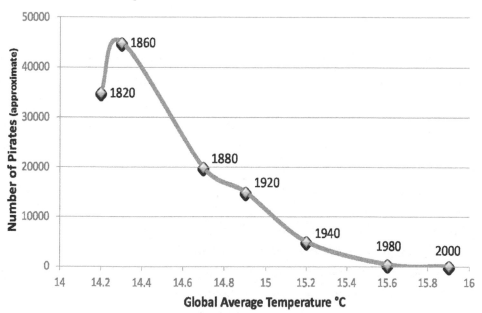

Source: Venganza.org

Dilbert also reminds us that confusing causation with correlation can lead to erroneous conclusions.[9]

Dilbert The Statistician

This is child's play, right? Wrong. We have seen numerous situations where professionals forgot this and did not question the causal link.

A consulting team was working with an Asian packaged goods manufacturer. The client wanted to know how to increase sales. The team had done exhaustive analysis on the available data and proudly shared one of their key conclusions: sales would increase if the client obtained (bought) more shelf space. The support for this was a clear correlation between sales and shelf space.

Good analysis but wrong conclusion—they got the causation backward. It is more sales that leads to more shelf space, not vice versa. Why? Because grocers do not want to lose sales by being out of stock of a product, so as sales go up, they allocate more shelf space to a product. Buying more shelf space (retailers will also give you more if you pay them to do so) is not likely to increase sales, but selling more will get you more shelf space.

This was not the only time we have seen intelligent people forget that

---

9.   DILBERT © 2011 Scott Adams. Used By permission of ANDREWS MCMEEL SYNDICATION. All rights reserved.

correlation is not causation. Where this caution is particularly important to keep in mind is when there is correlation but the causality is linked to a third variable, to which many things correlate. When looking at correlated data, always remember to consider if there is an untracked variable driving both.

This point is a bigger problem in the age of the internet because with massive data sets, it is even easier to find misleading correlations (such as the pirates and global warming). Given enough data, you will find lots of correlations. We saw one piece of analysis that was trying to understand location data, it discussed the overlap of people who were near McDonald's with people who were near mosques. We were not sure what to make of this and neither were they. In the end, it was probably just irrelevant.

31

What Doesn't Necessarily Tell You *Why*

Market research needs big data to more accurately understand customer behaviors; big data needs market research to understand why customers behave as they do.

Customer analytics and market research are often thought of as distinct functions and are usually managed separately, at times in different parts of the organization. While they do have their unique aspects, we think of them as flip sides of the same coin or pieces of a puzzle—both are about understanding consumers and helping companies uncover consumer-driven opportunities.

Market research uses self-reported data to understand consumer behavior. But this data is notoriously inaccurate. People will answer the questions about how many flights they took, how many were for leisure or business, and what class they flew, but their memory is not accurate. This is where big data can help by assembling more accurate behavioral data. We don't have to ask you how often you use Facebook, we can look at your data to know this. We don't have to ask you how often you shop in a particular grocery store and what categories and products you bought, your loyalty card data tells us this.

However, what the data doesn't tell us is why you chose that product nor what you thought of it. You might fly one airline because it is the cheapest or because you want the miles or because you have no choice as your company's travel policies mandate with whom you fly. This data is best obtained with surveys and other tools that interact directly with the customer.

At SingTel we organized the Living Analytics team to mix these two functions, and we believe the synergy worked.

For example, our understanding of recommendation engines was substantially enhanced through traditional qualitative research. We had consumers use a mocked-up restaurant selection site to understand how well a new recommendation engine worked. This gave us important feedback on the user experience. More importantly, we gained a crucial insight that the true competitor was not other restaurant selection sites but Google. We learned consumers preferred to search on Google and then go directly to the relevant restaurant pages on our site, giving us page views, but bypassing the search page (which was where most of the revenue was generated).

Another reason to marry big data and consumer research is to understand if we are accurately understanding the output.

We tested one location product that claimed to deliver a marketing message to customers as they entered a mall. No sign-in was required, the service geo-fenced the mall and then identified which of a telco's customers had entered that area. This triggered an SMS with a message the mall wanted to deliver (welcome, special offers, etc.). But did it work? Via our insight community (Chapter 44), we asked for people who would be going to that mall over a weekend and asked those who said yes to expect a message. The results indicated that those who got the message were indeed at the mall (a few got it driving nearby) and no one received the message who was not close by. All good. But the testing surfaced a problem: only half of the people who went to the mall received a message. Upon probing, the service admitted they had a capacity issue and only with our research were we able to dimension the substantial problem this caused.

THE LOCATION OF THE ANALYST MATTERS ALSO

A footnote to this case emphasizes the need for local insight. We personally tested the service on a Thursday night and didn't receive any messages. When we reported this, we were told the geo-fence was turned off at 6pm, when the mall closed. Stores in Australia are not open most weeknights but Thursday is late shopping night and the mall is open until 9pm. A team sitting in San Francisco wouldn't understand this, a local would.

Some will maintain that we just need enough customer data and traditional research will become unnecessary. But we disagree because often there are competing, different interpretations of why people behave as they do, or what actually happened—something traditional research is pretty good at surfacing.

32

The Three Ts—
Targeted, Tailored, Timely

Sending the wrong message at the wrong time often negates the impact of good targeting. Communications should be well targeted and relevant, which is to say, tailored and timely.

That communications and offers should be targeted is common wisdom. The era of mass marketing is supposedly over, and marketers are inclined to use the various tools available to them to narrowcast instead of broadcast. This is often the case. You can make almost infinite selections of criteria in sending an advertisement via Google or Facebook.

Targeting is good, but needs to be done well: bad targeting is probably worse than no targeting at all. Why? Because it irritates customers, which cannot be a good thing.

As we write this, we have received an email from Cathay Pacific on discount fares to the United States for people aged 65 and over. They may have targeted the offer to those who travel to the United States, but we doubt it. They do not seem to use their customer information very well, as they surely know we are not yet 65 (they have all our demographic information and reconfirm our dates of birth every time we fly) and therefore we are ineligible for this fare. Rather than delivering effective marketing, they have just annoyed us with another irrelevant message.

Unfortunately, they are not alone. Most of the messages we receive seem designed for someone else. But doing better is possible.

Tesco in the UK uses their Clubcard data to personalize coupons sent to

British customers. They claim to have millions of variations among the categories, brands, and coupon values that they offer. They credit Clubcard with a big role in their becoming the number one British grocer in 1996. While we have not done an exhaustive survey, Clubcard customers whom we have spoken to seem to agree. When we cite the value of their tailored approach, we often get nods of approval and more from their customers. Several said they eagerly await these mailings because they expect them to be something they will like. We believe that marketers who consistently deliver tailored messages to the right target will see strong responses.

We've seen this in action using big data. A cable TV provider was adding 40 new stations to their offering and their base ad was typical mass marketing—they sent everyone an email saying "We have 40 new stations! Here they are. Please sign up." But consumers don't want to sort through choices, they want to be showed what is relevant to them. So, when we built a model that predicted which of the five most popular stations a customer might like, we more than tripled the response rate. This targeting was only effective because we also changed from one message to five different ones that said "We now have Channel X!" providing the channel we predicted they preferred at the top of the email, then listing the other 39 new channels further down.

Keep in mind, targeting and tailoring do not need to be complex to provide customer value, nor do they require extensive data.

Working with a concert promotion agency in Philadelphia, we obtained substantial increases in response rates when we leveraged just one piece of customer information: email addresses tied to the major universities. How? We extracted information after the @ symbol, e.g. @upenn.edu, @temple.edu, @drexel.edu, to segment customers and provide relevant, tailored concert promotion messages.

However, tailoring only works if you send multiple offers. If you target just one offer, you avoid people you should not reach. Your response rate goes up, but your total responses go down because you are reaching fewer people overall. But if you send a second, more appropriate message to those screened out of the first offer, you get more responses, and likewise with the third and fourth offers. The more finely you slice your targets, the more you can send appropriate offers, the higher your total responses.

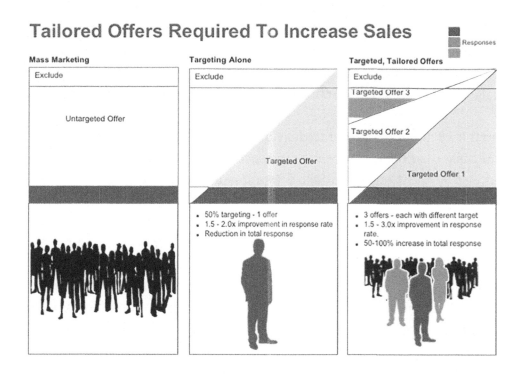

Tailored Offers Required To Increase Sales

Going back to the cable TV example, if we had only sent one message to those likely to subscribe to one channel, we would have a higher response rate but fewer responses. By sending one of six messages to everyone (five to each of the targeted channels, one default offer to everyone else) we increased both the response rates and the total number of responses.

As a side note, if we had better long-term attrition data, we would have identified a seventh segment of people to whom we shouldn't send anything as they would be annoyed by our marketing. There are no immediate lost sales to this group but, over time, we weaken our brand with these customers by over-marketing and threaten what business we do have with them. Most marketers have their do-not-contact list due to regulatory requirements, but few are able to add names to this list based on customer retention propensities.

SingTel's SMS advertising provides a clear example: it has the ability to target text messages to customers using demographics and other customer information but often fails to do so. SingTel was happy to sell untargeted texts that went to all customers. Consequently, we would receive text offers for discounts from nail salons, for which we are not a likely target. Over time, we chose to just ignore any text sent from SingTel.

The third T, timely, is harder to deliver. Although it is easier now in the age of mobile marketing, where we can reach you not only wherever you are, but also at most any time. Still, figuring out when to deliver an offer or message is not easy.

Some marketers do work against this dimension. When Mike's first two sons were born in New York, he and his wife received a sample pack of diapers and wipes in the hospital. Clearly a child's birth, especially a first child, is the time when parents are considering their preferences for baby products.

But many other marketing campaigns could be timely, if they took the effort. Years ago, in a workshop with Ford, we were discussing targeted, tailored, and timely marketing. Automotive companies are among the biggest marketing spenders and yet most of what they do is still mass marketing or shades of mass. They spend cumulatively thousands of dollars per vehicle on TV advertising and other media. Thousands more is spent on temporary price incentives.

They could do better. For example, in our meeting they pointed out that they knew exactly the time to sell a minivan to potential owners. When? When the third child was born (or second if the family had a live-in nanny). Why? Because for the third child, if all the children sit in the back row of a sedan, they are too close and that leads to fighting. But with a minivan, they have a second row of seats, so all three kids can be separated. Mike agreed this was true; he bought a Windstar minivan just before his third child arrived.

How could this information be better used to sell minivans? By reaching out to families with a third child on the way or newly arrived and letting the family experience the peace and quiet of a minivan, perhaps by offering a loaner car for free for a weekend. Now, offering anyone a free car for a weekend would be expensive, too expensive for mass marketing, but if well targeted, it might have a much higher return than mass marketing spending.

In the era of big data, you can become even more timely. If you drive a lot and are thus of interest to gas station marketers, it is possible to deliver the message just before your usual drive time, whether that is the morning and early evening, or, if you work the evening shift, then late afternoon and early the next morning. This is when you are most open to using an offer, so the response rate and impact should be higher (but please, no texting while driving).

USAA, a US based financial services company, has been a master for many decades of using the three Ts. Historically, their response rates were orders of magnitude higher than others because they delivered targeted, tailored and timely communications—such that customers lookedforward to receiving them.

Do all three Ts well and you build very strong relationships.

EXTENDING A SEGMENTATION TO AN ENTIRE CUSTOMER BASE

We are often asked how to link research-driven segment membership to a client's full customer list to allow segment-driven targeting. There are three ways to do this:

1. Create product/service variations that allow the consumer to self-target
2. Use your sales force
3. Use your data

1. Create product/service variations that allow the consumer to self-target

This is the traditional model and still valid when you have only a few segments. For example, a mobile phone company creates several models with different features, or a credit card company offers several different types of card: American Express has their blue, green, gold and black cards, each with a clear value proposition targeted at a different segment and marketed so that customers can self-select the card best fit for their segment.

2. Use your sales force

You can educate your sales force about the segments, how to identify them and what offer each segment should consequently receive. One of our favorite examples comes from B2B telco modeling. We're simplifying things a bit, but they needed to deliver a price offer to some customers but a higher margin reliability offer to others. Sales forces often default to pricing offers as they are easier to sell, but this needed to be avoided. A driving variable of the price/reliability segmentation was the reporting structure of the telco manager: did he or she work for the CIO or CFO? Work for the CIO and we should focus on quality (because the CIO wants redundancy and reliability to avoid network outages), work for the CFO and pricing is more important.

With just this simple but reliable insight, the sales force became more confident in selling higher margin products to quality-sensitive managers rather than selling everyone the default option, which was a lower margin package, designed for price-sensitive customers.

Another example was for a bank, which developed a set of four questions for their mortgage sales force to ask customers so that they could suggest appropriate, but higher margin, products to customers. The questions made it comfortable for the sales force to sell these products because the questions not only identified the non-price sensitive customers but also made it more comfortable for them to pitch the higher margin products.

3. Use your data

Build predictive models: one of our favorite uses of a model to provide actionable predictions comes from Capital One. They described how they used data to predict the purpose of a customer's call. Instead of offering annoying menus of choices, they identified the caller based on their phone number, predicted the reason for the call and then diverted the caller directly to the appropriate department. They said they got it 70 percent right (and otherwise the call center operator would quickly divert the caller to the right department).

In sum, if you want to target your tailored offers, use one of these three approaches—there aren't any others.

33

Big Segments Still Matter!

Drive targeting and messaging with hundreds of micro segments but use larger, macro segments for product and value proposition development.

With the ability to create hundreds or thousands of micro segments, targeted at a hundred or fewer people, is traditional market segmentation still necessary or is it an anachronism?

While we believe marketers should use micro segments to develop and test different offers or communications, we think this falls mostly in the realm of tactical marketing: what price, which of different incentives, what color, what wording, and so on. These are good things to do, part of making offers and messages relevant.

But what micro segmentation does not do well is suggest what should be there that is not. It does not identify white spaces or new product opportunities other than to classify some people as non-responders to the current set of tactical offers and messages.

For that, you still need macro segments, the four, five, six or so segments created from needs and behaviors. These large segments can provide insight via in-depth analysis and follow-on qualitative work into unmet needs. For example, you could assemble a focus group based on a specific segment and then use the *category problem analysis* process (discussed in Chapter 12) to uncover problems and unmet needs.

For several financial institutions, we've conducted segmentation work aimed at developing new value propositions for underserved market segments. A traditional view is that the more affluent a person is, the more they need and want sophisticated financial products and financial advice. Basic banking provides CDs (certificate of deposit or term deposit) for the mass market, stocks and bonds for the affluent, and private equity for the wealthy. What segmentation demonstrated is that there are opportunities for propositions that are off that linear relationship of wealth and complexity. There are the less affluent who would value the product mix and services of the affluent and may be prepared to pay for it (via fees rather than embedded into products) and conversely, there are affluent individuals who want basic products and not a highly educated financial advisor.

This example oversimplifies the specific work, but makes the broader point that only with traditional segmentation will you understand these more strategic opportunities; tactical marketing of current offers will not surface them.

34

Location, Location, Location

We believe the value in location data comes from analyzing patterns; we often find that patterns are more telling than single events or locations.

When we started working at Singtel, we observed that much work was being done using single point location data to target relevant advertisements. Thinking about how to derive more actionable insight from this data, we shifted the focus from single points (Where am I right now?) to patterns (Where have I been over time?).

Why would location *patterns* deliver more insight?

1.   Decisions are rarely made in real time
2.   One-off location data is messy and potentially misleading
3.   Patterns provide actionable insight into user behaviors
4.   Understanding patterns helps to avoid frustrating users

First, many decisions are not made in real time. This limits our ability to use location to influence customer decisions.

We observed this when studying dining out. There are numerous apps that help you locate nearby places to eat. Some people do decide at the last moment. But when we surveyed diners in Singapore about where they ate dinner last night, most indicated that they chose the location the day before, not just as they headed out to eat. What they used the location apps for was to reconfirm the address of the restaurant or to check for deals before walking in. But the decision of where to eat was not influenced much by their location-based, last-minute search.

To the same point, when a colleague suggested we could use location data to determine if you were at a car dealer and then deliver automotive ads, we felt that was too late. By the time you are at the dealer, the opportunity for ads to shift your purchase is likely small. Data should be used to reach consumers before or as they make a decision, not afterwards.

Second, one-off location data is messy and potentially misleading; looking at patterns provides a less ambiguous picture.

Unless you check in, the location data from your phone does not provide enough accuracy to deliver a relevant message. This is especially true in vertical, mixed-use areas, because location data is two-, not three-dimensional. We may know you are near a certain location, but we cannot tell if you are in the shopping mall on the lower floors, working in the office building on the higher floors, or staying in the hotel or residences on the top floors. We also ran various tests using network data, and often two people in the same room or apartment would be picked up by different wireless towers that suggested different locations for them. This is why so many apps want you to check in; it is the only reliable way (right now) to know exactly where you are.

Third, analyzing patterns provides more actionable insight into user behaviors.

Imagine you are at work and you walk outside the office for five minutes and then return inside. Maybe you were having something delivered, maybe you were giving something to someone else, or maybe you were meeting a customer to escort him or her inside. Or, maybe due to poor-quality data, you actually just went from one place in the building to another, never going outside. It could be many things. Now, imagine I see that same thing happen four times a day, every day. What does this tell me? Likely, you are a smoker. The pattern is more telling than the single event.

Google has apparently understood the value of location patterns. In developing features for their mapping applications, they tested using location pattern to identifying streets to avoid when looking for a parking spot. For this, the mapping application tracks areas where cars circle a block several times, not just once, i.e. a pattern. Go around once and maybe you dropped someone off, overshot your destination or one of many other potential explanations. Do it repeatedly and consistently and you're probably having trouble finding a parking spot.[10]

In work with location data, our team surfaced many interesting patterns. There were people who frequently traveled on business, those who drove their cars a lot, those who frequently ate out or drank on weekdays, those who went home every night, and those who exhibited many other behaviors.

Why is this helpful? Based on a pattern, you can target a relevant (and often timely) message. For example, if you frequently dine out on weekdays (when restaurants and bars have excess capacity), we can encourage a restaurant to send you an offer to entice you to try their food, or a bar can offer you a free beer. At the same time, you can suggest to Pizza Hut that they target the stay-at-home crowd, for whom restaurant and bar offers

Big Data Example – Leveraging Location Patterns

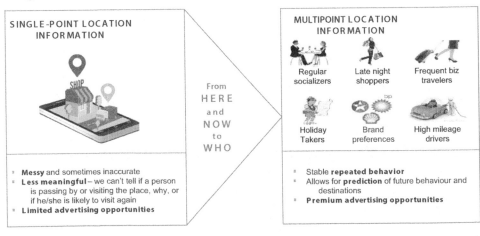

---

are not of interest.

Fourth, understanding the pattern may also help you avoid frustrating users.

Many applications use annoying captchas to predict whether a user is real or a bot.[11] However, by watching how the user scrolls across the page, we can infer the same identify information, as humans and bots do not move the cursor in the same patterns. Since users are not notified when the prediction is made, the use of the pattern data can entirely remove an inconvenient login process.

We wish more companies would review similar scroll patterns from their customers. When using Quora, a question and answer application, we often accidentally hit the home button, moving back to the start of an article. Noticing the behavior of repeatedly scrolling to the top of an article, then instantly manually scrolling back to the prior position should tell us that the information on the application should be reorganized or that the initial scroll was an unintended behavior.

The same frustration applies to text messages. When living in Singapore, we would bicycle past Changi airport every Sunday morning and received two messages urging us to sign up for a mobile phone roaming service. An analysis of the pattern would have indicated someone does not fly out twice within an hour and doesn't need the second message, a more detailed analysis might also suggest no need for the first message either. We were annoyed two times each week, airline employees probably received the message every day as they arrived at work.

Our experience illustrates searching for patterns can yield valuable insights.

---

11.   Source: https://www.google.com/recaptcha/intro/v3beta.html

THINK STRATEGICALLY

Leveraging proprietary data can be the difference between good results and winning results.

Phone companies have a competitive advantage in collecting location pattern data. While location data is available from multiple sources, telecoms are unique in their ability to capture location patterns. Thus, it is in the interest of the phone company to capture and use this data; if it provides insight, it becomes unique to the phone company and consequently a source of competitive advantage.

The same point can be made for retailers in using their product-level purchase data or financial institutions using their transaction data. It is better to develop useful insights with data you have that others cannot get than to build your insights from data that others can access, which means they can copy your findings, unless there is substantial first-mover advantage.

35
Behavioral Models Rule

Models are the drivers behind successful CRM (Customer Relationship Management) targeting. The most impactful, actionable ones leverage behavioral data and downplay demographics.

Too much marketing still relies on demographics. Communications are still largely placed based on age, income and gender. Using demographics is better than pure mass marketing, but in the age of big data, we can do better by paying attention to behaviors over demographics.

It is easy to challenge demographics. When talking to students we make the point that they are demographically similar. Similar age, similar income, similar education, etc. We then go around the room and ask either what car they drive or what shampoo they use. The results vary considerably. Thus, using their similar demographics would be of little use in predicting their product preferences.

Increasing Value Of Customer Data

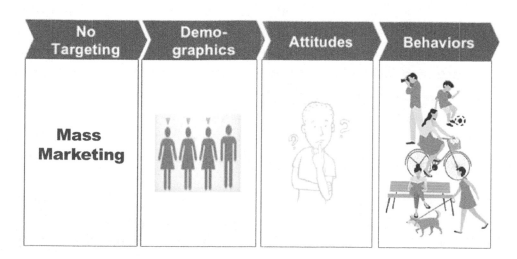

Successful modeling usually begins with a propensity model, that is, a model built to predict someone's propensity to own or use a product. These are best done by looking at behaviors, e.g. what products they own, how they use those products. We previously shared (see Chapter 26) how we used calls made at a specific time of day to identify price-sensitive customers. The full model relied on that behavior as well as the number of calls made, the number of callers, use of international calling and other behaviors. Demographics added a small amount of value to the model, but not much, even though we had extensive demographic information. (Also, behavioral data is usually cleaner, as it is internally generated. Demographic data can be messier as it is often manually collected.

Big data has provided new sources of data that allow building better and more valuable models.

For instance, at one telco, we used call data records (CDRs) to identify missing demographic characteristics for prepaid customers (about whom little was known) which lead to increased advertising sales. CDRs are a wonderful source of predictive information. Who we call, how often, and how long we talk all exhibit patterns that can be useful. In this case, by looking at who called whom, we could accurately predict gender, age and affluence.

Visa introduced us to a company that combined CDRs from a South American telco with credit information on small consumer loans to create a credit score. This was invaluable in extending micro credit. Most potential loan customers lacked the traditional information needed to score them. Yet, the loan losses were too high to provide loans without some scoring. CDR-based behavior models addressed this problem. As a bonus, the loans were often used to pay the mobile phone bill, so the telco not only made money from selling credit scoring data but also in its core business.

However, models must be used properly, not wishfully—that is, for the intended audience and offer. There are no universal models. While building CRM capability in Australia, our SME team created a very good targeting model for a "product of the month" outbound calling campaign. We tested, via our call center, our ability to focus the calling on customers more likely to buy that product. The model worked: testing revealed that high propensity customers were more likely to buy than medium propensity customers and low propensity customers were even less likely to buy. Exactly what we wanted so going forward we could call those more likely to make a purchase and not annoy those who were uninterested in the offer.

However, lacking time and resources, the team used the very same model the next month even though the product for that month was different. This time the results were poor.

What was interesting in this case is that, because the offer was sold via a call center, if the monthly special offer was declined, the phone rep could sell the customer anything else. So we asked the team to see how sales of the previous month's product were among this month's customers. Guess what? Sales were quite good for the previous month's product, which shouldn't have been surprising as they were using a targeting model built for that product, not the current month's product.

The moral of this story must surely be: when you try and sell what *you* want to sell, people may not buy. When you try to sell what *they* are interested in, they probably will buy.

UNINTENDED MODELING BIAS

One danger in building any type of modeling is to beware of unintended bias in selecting your data. This is described very well by Cathy O'Neil in Weapons of Math Destruction *and also Malcolm Kendrick's* Doctoring Data. *They both illustrate that data is not automatically pure and unbiased: in evaluating a data set you need to make sure there isn't built-in bias. Crime prevention models aim to focus policing resources in the areas where they can do the most to reduce crime. But those models rely on reported crime data—put more police officers in an area and they'll probably notice more crime, especially petty crime like traffic violations. So the model will reinforce the bias of the person staffing the police and may ignore neighborhoods with equally frequent petty crime that goes unreported.*

This concern is more serious when we think about new-age techniques like machine learning. The computer doesn't understand bias and assumes the historic data is sufficient to make accurate, unbiased predictions, even if it isn't. This can hamper needed change. For example, historically, women have been paid less than men. A machine learning model would therefore look at this data and assume that women will accept lower salaries than men, even though this may not be desirable (or legal). Machine learning, in essence, reinforces the past and resists change.

Of course, bias is not limited to machine learning. John Stewart, former host of the Daily Show, *makes a similar point about his own bias with a relevant story about how he unintentionally hired "white dudes from Harvard" despite believing he was unbiased about race, gender and education.*

36

Reduce Churn, Don't Cause It!

Building a churn model is easy. The challenge is building a model that helps reduce churn, not just predicts it.

Churn (also known as attrition) is an industry term that refers to customers who leave for a competitor. Financial modelers appreciate models that predict who is likely to churn and thus the aggregate level of churn. This helps them make better financial predictions. However, the marketing team's objective is not just to measure churn but to reduce it. They don't need to know who will churn. They need to predict for whom they can reduce the likelihood of churn and what intervention would lead to that reduction.

Many churn models are useless. The statistics are valid but there is no connection between the model and marketing actions, so they have no impact. The most egregious example we experienced was at one telco where we were asked if we could improve the churn model. "Yes," we answered, "but to do that, can you tell us how the model is used?" The answer was, "Not much." At that company, every customer with an expiring contract was called with a renewal offer. Everyone got the same offer. If they didn't renew, they were called a second time the same month with the same offer: everyone, the same offer. If they still didn't renew, they were called a third time: again, everyone, the same offer. How was the model used? If the team ran out of calling capacity, they would use the churn model to select who got the third call. So the model only influenced who got a third call, it was not used for the first and second calls, which was the bulk of the calling. Improving a model used only in that way would have little impact, regardless of the accuracy of the model.

Churn models need to reflect the likely actions marketers will take. Some customers are loyal, love your service, love your network, and are very unlikely to churn. Acknowledge their loyalty. Appreciate them. Or just leave them be. But don't harass them about renewal and don't waste money contacting them, you'll more likely annoy them than delight them.

Some customers are inertial; they are passively loyal. They just don't want to bother with considering changes. Particularly for this type of customer, avoid contacting them. The impact is more likely negative: "Oh, my contract is up? Maybe I have to look at alternatives."

Some customers hate you. They are mentally gone, they just need the contract end-date to avoid switching penalties. Leave them be. You're unlikely to change their intention, so all you do is waste your money contacting them, especially calling, which is expensive. One model identified these people by looking at a rapid decline in calling volume—they had already gotten a new phone number and were using it; it was too late to save them, they had left.

It is the customers in between that a churn model should focus on. The model should first predict risk of churning and then among those at risk, identify who might respond to what offer. This leads the effort to "Show me the money." At one telco, the modeling was competitor-sensitive: they predicted not only who might churn, but which of two competitors they would churn to. This allowed sending out offers tailored to the particular competitor, addressing their strengths relative to the competitor. This worked much better than a generic approach.

For another telco, we had a group of high-risk, high-value customers. We tested a birthday cake offer. (All customers got a happy birthday email; for this group we upped the investment, delivering a cake, usually to their office.) Evaluating the responses, we saw that this extra spending was justified for women, but not men. This allowed the client to focus their churn spending where it worked and look for other offers for those with whom it was ineffective.

Churn modeling is like many analytic tools: you must first think about how to use them to achieve business impact and then focus your analysis and output on capturing that value instead of creating an interesting, or even accurate, but academic model.

37
Media Still Matters

Make sure your advertisements fit the media channel, as not all messages work in every environment.

When selecting a channel for marketing content, it is worth questioning whether the content matches the media. We would not place the same advertisements in *The Economist* as on MTV. Yet, somehow with the proliferation of new media channels, this fundamental idea of matching messaging to the media is often lost. To ensure a message has the intended impact, think of how it is received by the audience.

Many advertisers understand that online music streaming services such as Pandora and Spotify are similar to radio, and treat the audio, not the video, as the central media for their message. Instead, some inappropriately repurpose television advertisements, leading to wasted advertising spend by their failure to tell us what they are selling.

Consider the following advertisement, transcribed below, that we heard repeatedly on Pandora while commuting to work:

> *"The most important thing in life will always be family. The people right there, right now."*
>
> *Background audio: Beeping and clicking sounds*
>
> *"Dominic Toretto, you don't know me; you're about to."*
>
> *Background audio: Beep, beep, loud explosion*
>
> *"Looks like the sons of London have followed us home. Remember Owen Shaw. This is his big bad brother."*
>
> *"We're being hunted."*

Background audio: Gun reloading

"I am going with you."

Background audio: Car engine, explosion

"One last ride. Daddy's got to go to work."

Background audio: Machine gun; glass shattering and an explosion

"This takes crazy to a whole other level, whoa!"

Background audio: Glass shatters; a single gunshot and explosion; two seconds of classical music; another explosion; car tires screeching and more glass shattering

"Rated PG-13."

When streaming music on a cell phone, there are few reasons to look at the screen. The phone often is in our pocket while listening to music. Thus, the transcribed audio above matched our entire advertising experience, which begs the question, what is this advertisement promoting?

The PG-13 rating indicates a movie, but which one, and how confident are you in your answer? Maybe you recognize the movie because you are a fan of the series and are familiar with the character names. More likely, you are like us and are unsure of what product is being advertised from the dialogue alone. (Sorry, but to make the point, we are not going to tell you what the advertisement was for but you can google the words to find out yourself; something a company wouldn't normally ask of its customers.)

It's not enough for media to be relevant for a channel. It also must be targeted to the customer, so it is necessary to check if different channels attract different customers.

One client at an apparel company had recently added an online presence. The transition had gone seemingly well; website traffic was increasing. Yet sales were flat. The client was perplexed: why were website views so impressive, but sales so disappointing?

With years of experience with in-store sales, the marketing team had a strong message that worked for traditional retail channels (e.g. newspaper, magazines). Like most companies, they wanted to start an online channel and to accelerate the process, they repurposed the existing advertising messages into online ads. The problem was that online they were reaching a different audience for whom the advertisements didn't work.

Expanding to the new channel, the assumption was that online offerings would increase the reach for the same customer; however, the missed realization was that the retail and online customers were not one and the same. The online store opened up a new channel for people that would never walk into the stores. These customers had different motivations— often they were shopping to buy gifts for others. Thus, the retail media messaging did not match these customers' shopping intent.

It goes to show that messaging should reflect the channel and be created for the customer.

AIMLESS MARKET RESEARCH

In the last example, having dissimilar customers on the online channel should not have been a surprise because the client had evidence that the established customer persona for the advertisements did not apply to online customers. A survey conducted months earlier had indicated that online customers had different shopping intentions from those of retail customers. Yet, the data was never effectively put into use. Upon probing, it was unclear why the survey was created except generically to learn something interesting about the customer. Like so much market research, if it does not start with an appropriate question, the insight will never deliver value.

38

The Inaccuracy Of Personalized Predictions

Delivering truly personalized recommendations is hard. Done right— which is difficult—it can drive sales. Done poorly, it can annoy and drive away customers.

On vacation with a friend, we got a massage at an upscale resort's spa. At the beginning of the massage, the masseuses asked if we wanted them to focus on any specific area. One of us said the lower back, the other, the neck. So we had the promise of a more personalized massage, tailored to our requests. Because we were in the same room, it was evident that the masseuses proceeded to deliver exactly the same massage to each of us; each of them operated as an echo of the other, moving from one step to another with almost identical timing. If this was synchronized swimming, they would have won an award, but they certainly did not win any awards from us for responding to our requests. The massage was good, but generic; having created an expectation of personalization, it fell short when this promise was not fulfilled. It would have been better to not promise personalization at all.

Understanding the power of personalization has led to the increased use of recommendation engines—software that asks or infers our preferences and then promises to respond with more relevant recommendations. With the increase of data sources and computing power, many people expect that more and more of what we like or do can be predicted.

But recommendation engines are hard to develop and deploy. Amazon uses not one engine, but several, to deliver their results because they could not find a good, single approach. If you look at their site you'll even see that they offer multiple forms of the output to customer:

- Sponsored products related to this item (Things I want to sell to you)
- Customers who bought this item also bought … (What else might you want to buy?)
- Customers who viewed this item but bought … instead (Perhaps you'd like to buy this instead?)
- Customers who viewed this item also viewed … (I'm just trying to keep you on my site!)

Delivering on the promise of personalization is not easy.

Generally, there are two approaches to getting it right: collaborative filtering (recommendations from similar users) or content-based filtering (recommendations from similar products).

In the movie-viewing space, ThinkAnalytics has created a collaborative filtering recommendation engine that ingests viewing habits and looks for users that enjoy similar content (you like X, she likes X and Y, so maybe you would like Y). Several leading cable TV providers have installed ThinkAnalytics' approach and seen significant increases in acceptance of the recommendations, along with the consequent increase in viewership.

Jinni, an Israeli company, takes a different approach: content-based filtering. They invested in detailed, content-driven data, creating hundreds (thousands?) of meta tags to help them understand why you like what you watch. This is then used to suggest what else you might like (you like movies with middle-aged, female heroines, so you might like these movies that also feature middle-aged, female heroines).

But successfully deploying personalization is not easy.

Netflix ran a competition a few years ago to improve the recommendations they provide on shows you might like to watch. Despite a million-dollar prize, the results were only marginally better than their existing approach, and the winning approach was so complicated they chose not to deploy it.

We have tested several restaurant recommendation engines, designed to help find new eateries someone might like, but most approaches have failed. During one test, we asked for recommendations for an Italian restaurant and one option was for a Japanese restaurant. Upon digging, we could see how that came about—the restaurant served "Japanese pizza." But this was so far afield from what we expected that in real life we would have just ignored a clearly aberrant suggestion.

While we experience successful personalization from many online services (Facebook tells us about our friends, not everyone; Google tailors searches based on previous information we've shared), unfortunately much online marketing seems to fail in delivering relevant personalization.

When we ask audiences if, knowing how much information companies have about us, do they experience "personalized, relevant" advertising, the universal answer is no. The more common answer is that much of what they receive is closer to spam.

We've all had this happen. We search for something on the web, we buy it and for a long period afterward we get ads for that product that we are no longer looking for, as we own it. This is not just annoying, it is destructive of brand relationships as it triggers buyer's remorse, that is second guessing a decision you've made and can't correct.

One time, we checked in at a bus station, so there was no ambiguity about the location. However, we were served an ad for Shell gasoline. Not really appropriate when boarding a bus.

This lack of personalization happens because programmatic media buying (the process of placing most ads on the web) too often relies on either demographics (which are blunt targeting tools, as discussed earlier) or search data (which is called remarketing, that is sending you messages about exactly what you searched for). What they don't use is purchase data, which is hidden behind https security and so not available to use in targeting.

What doesn't happen, but should, is using data to develop an actionable prediction of what we might find relevant outside of an immediate purchase or average demographics. Over time, with more tools and better data (and more savvy media buyers), we'll be better able to deliver more relevant and personalized messaging, but until then, be careful that your targeting is working and not annoying.

BUILDING A RECOMMENDATION ENGINE

While the devil is in the detail, the basics behind developing a recommendation engine are quite simple to comprehend.

Wonkish alert.

Imagine, we wanted to create a content-based recommendation system. We have text on restaurant reviews. We can transform this text into a structured numeric data set by counting how many times each word shows up in the review text. In the below diagram, we might pretend that word1 = 'drinks', word2 = 'atmosphere', and word3 = 'tasty'—of course when looking at all the distinct words found in full restaurant reviews, there would be tens of thousands of different columns.

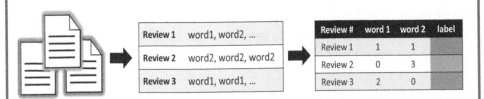

Once structured in this format, it is possible to plot each review. For simplicity, we have only plotted each review by word1 and word2.

Review #	word 1	word 2	label
Review 1	1	1	
Review 2	0	3	
Review 3	2	0	

After plotting, all that is left is to calculate is the distance between the reviews. The assumption here is that restaurant reviews that use similar text are more like each other. There are numerous ways to determine similarity—we showed the angle between the reviews and the shortest line to connect the reviews below. The same expansion of choices applies to the prior steps as well, in which the most advanced recommendation engines use more robust statistics than just counting the occurrence of words.

Using this data, we can infer that reviews that are closer to each other

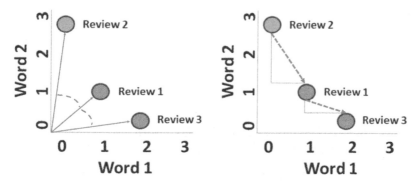

are more similar. Review 3 is more similar to Review 1 than Review 2 because they are closer. Thus, we can use the reviews from one restaurant to find other similar restaurants, and decide to recommend them based on if a user likes or dislikes the restaurant with the original review.

39

Ignorant Competitive Pricing Is An Oxymoron

Price sensitivity is often overstated; while people say they buy based on price, they often lack the information to do so.

Pricing theory makes a key assumption that is often wrong. It assumes we have complete information. We rarely, if ever, do. For major purchases we may do more research, but even when we buy a house, we have only partial information about what is for sale, the pricing, and the terms that have an impact on the price. For everyday purchases, we often have in mind what are known as key value indicators or KVIs. It may be the price of a gallon of gas or a two-liter Coke. But that covers only a small portion of the 30,000 items in a typical grocery store and of those items we buy.

To address this we have many times employed a simple set of pricing questions to ferret out those products for which competitive pricing and demand curves will be misleading. Before determining price elasticity ask:

1. What is the usual price of the product?
2. How confident are you that this is correct?
3. What is the usual price of competitive products?
4. How confident are you that this is correct?

Only when the answers to questions 1 and 3 are accurate and 2 and 4 affirmative, do you have a situation where competitive pricing truly comes into play.

The four questions do need to be viewed in the context of the buying process. If you do not know the prices, but go to a price comparison site before making a purchase, then you are making an informed decision. But not everyone does that and not for all products. That is why some stores inhibit price discovery.

Go to the fresh cookie store in the mall, the one that uses a fan to entice you with the smell of freshly baked cookies. Do you know the price of a cookie? Unlikely. Do they want you to consider price before asking for a cookie for you and your kids? No. The pricing is often positioned on the sidewall of the shop, there to see, but not in your face.

On the same note, the next time you are in an upscale restaurant, take a closer look at the prices. Do you see dollar signs? Unlikely. By removing indicators such as currency symbols, we tend to lose the connection between the number and its meaning (cost).

A bank in the Philippines was rebalancing the pricing of their fees and services—rebalancing because they wanted to lower those fees that drove their price perception and raise those that did not. We asked the four questions for a variety of fees. It turned out there was one relatively frequently charged fee for which the four questions were far out of line. People were confident that they knew the price (questions 1 and 2). The problem? They were confidently stating a price that was three times the actual fee. They also were confident that their perceived price was competitive with other banks (questions 3 and 4).

What did the client do? Doubled the fee and advertised it, because it was perceived as a price reduction! You do not often get such situations, but when you do, they are golden.

So, remember, before getting into a complicated pricing study, check to see if your customers are accurately aware of your and your competitors' prices—if they aren't, standard pricing research results can be misleading.

BANK PRICING

While people will grouse about fees, there is a big difference between normal services and penalties. Why are bounced check fees or overdrafts so expensive? One reason is we are less sensitive to fees that are penalties—we feel we've done something wrong and therefore being "punished" is not out of line.

40
Land Ahoy! Set The Anchor

When customers have low price-awareness, anchoring and framing can influence their behavior.

Behavioral economics teaches us the importance of providing benchmarks. Dan Ariely, Professor of Psychology and Behavioral Economics at Duke University, has conducted numerous experiments showing that humans do not always make decisions in line with the traditional economic model. He has shown the existence of "arbitrary coherence," described as the following: "While initial prices are 'arbitrary,' once those prices are established in our minds they will shape not only present prices but also future prices (this makes them 'coherent')."

We are believers in this and have seen it work in action. Testing anchoring in the pricing strategy for a concert production company, we expanded the number of ticket offerings. Initially, only a single ticket was offered at a price of $39.99. We repositioned this as an early bird ticket (available until twenty-four hours before the concert) and added two new options. One addition was a regular ticket which was available the day of the concert, but provided the incentive for customers to make early purchases to save money. The other addition was a VIP ticket with few incremental benefits except moving to the front of the line when entering.

Concert Ticket Prices: VIP Price Provides Anchor

Ticket	Fare
VIP	79.99
Regular	43.99
Early bird	39.99

Not surprisingly, we did not sell many VIP tickets, but that was not the point. The VIP offer established an arbitrary comparison price, making the early bird ticket appear as a better deal than it was as a stand-alone offer. By adding two ticket options, each with clear positioning versus the previous single price, we saw sales exceed projections.

This doesn't just apply to pricing. The ideas are applicable any time you are setting expectations.

Customer Service is an example where arbitrary timelines can influence customer satisfaction. Tell a customer to expect a delivery in two days, but then show up in three and you will have angered the customer. If, instead, you had set an expected delivery date of four days, then the same three-day delivery will create customer delight. When customers lack a point of reference, anchoring and framing are useful tools to influence customer perceptions.

In setting your pricing in situations with low price-awareness, consider offering options that are designed to anchor and frame your value, guiding your customers to the preferred option

41
Kinky Pricing

Demand curves are not smooth; finding the inflection points (kinks) where price does influence demand is key to uncovering profit improvement opportunities.

Economists believe in nice, smooth demand curves. Many research tools do as well, based on the output they create. But that is not the reality: real demand curves have kinks, that is, steep upward parts connected to shallow, relatively flat parts. Knowing where these kinks are can help you set better pricing.

This was brought to life for us first when we did work looking at ketchup pricing. The client used Nielsen output to assess price elasticity and, therefore, to set the prices of their different sizes. But this output had two flaws: it was based on smooth demand curves and there was little variation in the price of ketchup over time, making the model output further suspect.

Our solution was to use a technique called brand-price trade-off or BPTO. In BPTO you show a respondent a shelf set with the relevant competitive brands and prices. The respondent looks at the shelf set and then picks the product they would buy. We then increase the price of the chosen item. The respondent again picks a product to buy. This time we find that they may choose the same product (they are brand and size loyal), or they choose a now relatively cheaper product, which could be a different size (still brand loyal), or they choose a different brand (a switcher).

Often, this information is input into a model that creates smoothed demand curves, which we believe to be a mistake. In this case, because each respondent went through more than two hundred choices (which went quickly; this was not a case of task overload) we did not need to model; we had the purchase intent for every brand at every needed price combination. So there was no modeling used.

Did this matter? Absolutely. We identified where the kinks were in the demand curve and set prices appropriately. This meant for one size, if you increased the price by 10 cents, there was a dramatic decrease in sales, but as the price increased further, there was a limited drop-off in sales. The client should either keep the price as is or increase it substantially, but to choose the middle ground was uneconomical.

Real Demand Curves Kinky, Not Curved

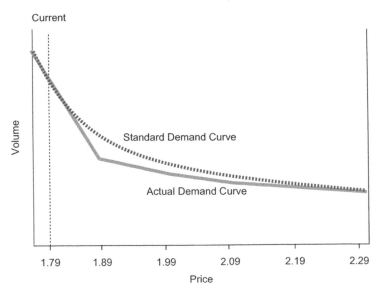

What made this work valuable was that the findings suggested big changes in the client's pricing. Previously, their pricing strategy supported small decreases in price per ounce as the sizes grew larger, that is, it rewarded consumers for buying more. Their new pricing strategy was much more flexible, reflecting kinks in the demand curve, so the price per ounce differences became much more pronounced. For example, the large bottles actually charged a premium over the smaller bottles. While this appeared to make no economic sense (one could just buy more of the smaller ones), the results held up in the real world when implemented, where we believed, first, few people are constantly scanning ketchup prices and second, if you use a lot of ketchup, you find larger bottles convenient, and so worth a premium.

We also demonstrated the opportunity to raise the price of the smallest bottle, which was price inelastic until it rose above that of the smallest competitive brand. We interpreted this to suggest that a segment was brand-insensitive and would simply buy the cheapest bottle, knowing they used little but wanted some in the house. This was important because grocery stores often carried only one brand's smallest bottle, stocking only larger sizes of competitors' brands. Again, by identifying the kink (the lowest competitive price), profitability was improved.

We were also able to show that there were clear packaging loyalties, with some consumers preferring glass (recyclers) while others liked plastic (moms with kids who liked to drop bottles). This suggested considering packaging preferences in setting prices, something that had not happened before.

We have had repeated success using BPTO in the form discussed above to show companies how to set more profitable prices—both in heavily promoted categories where price knowledge is likely high (like soda and bread) and in others where price knowledge is more sporadic. In all cases, we identified kinks that led to capturing pricing opportunities, sometimes by lowering price to grow unit sales despite lower margins, sometimes to lower sales but capture higher margins.

42

Size Matters

Spend more time with your most important customers.

Standard sales force strategy tells us to think of our clients along two dimensions: current value and potential value. A good sales force plan categorizes accounts, often grading accounts as A, B, and C or high, medium and small sales. The plan should also look at the future and assess if the account is likely to grow substantially, stay as is, or shrink. A manager can then create a grid as below, place all accounts into one of the nine resulting boxes, and ask if his or her team's sales efforts are in line with the indicated actions, that is, whether you are investing in growing large or medium accounts with potential, or spending too much time managing the status quo and spending time with low potential accounts.

Where To Focus Sales Efforts

Opportunity To Grow Sales

	Low	Medium	High
High (A accounts)			Spend more time here
Medium (B account)			
Low (C accounts)	Spend less time here		

Current sales level

At Synovate we learned we could do better in defining and using this matrix.

First, we underestimated the upside from large accounts. When asked to estimate their share of Client A's business, teams consistently overestimated their share. This led the team to underestimate the growth potential and focus more on servicing versus growing the accounts. In one market, the largest client was assessed with a 50 percent share, but when discussed with the client, we were closer to 25 percent. The growth potential of an already large client was three times what was previously contemplated. This led the location manager to assign additional resources, which resulted in capturing substantial new business.

Similarly, in another market, the team estimated their share of their largest client at 25 percent, but discussions with the client indicated it was about 5 percent. Again, this led the location manager to invest much more in that relationship, resulting in substantial sales growth.

The time and resources need to come from somewhere, and that should be from the small clients who offer limited upside even if they grow, and medium clients with limited upside. We should be nice to them, do good work, but our growth focus should be elsewhere.

And for really small, unattractive accounts or projects, we should decline because one big waste of time is writing proposals for accounts or projects that are unlikely to be profitable.

However, sometimes, when you have the discipline to turn down unattractive business, it becomes attractive. In Synovate Hong Kong, we wrote a "turn-down" letter, one that could politely suggest to a client that another firm was better placed to serve their project. It was a polite way to avoid winning C business.

Late one Friday, we came into the office and found the customer loyalty team leader, Mia Wong, still at work. When asked why, she said she had sent the turn-down letter and it had not worked. "How can it not work?" we asked. She related how she had sent the letter in response to a RFP (request for proposal) from a small company in a small market that had no research department. The RFP had come from someone who would not understand research well. Later, she received a call from the company's CEO, who said, "But you have to do this work for us. My friend, the CEO [of a larger local company] said you are the only firm to use for what we need." Accordingly, a lousy project for a C client became much more attractive because the client was now the CEO (uncommon in research) and was clearly uncompetitive (so the margins could be improved, making it a B project).

Take the time to accurately prioritize accounts; a little work can change who you focus on and deliver large sales increases.

43

Parents Don't Appreciate Leaky Diapers!

Product performance still matters: deliver fundamental product features before turning to differentiation.

It is true that more and more products are becoming commodities, or near commodities, a point made clear in the excellent book by Professor Youngme Moon of Harvard Business School, called *Different: Escaping the Competitive Herd*. Thus, the rise of generic and no-label brands in grocery stores or even no-label retailers, such as Aldi. However, this doesn't mean that all products are commodities or that product performance isn't important.

Working for a consumer products company in Korea, we were asked to help improve the company's disposable diaper marketing. They asked what would help most—better packaging, advertising, pricing, promotions, or distribution? While exploring these areas, one feature of the product became clear—the diapers leaked! This, of course, is the opposite of the fundamental product promise of diapers, and yet the company was not that concerned, saying that this always happened (with their product) and consumers did not mind. At that time, the company was insulated from international competition, but it was clear this would not last much longer. So, while we provided suggestions for improving their marketing, our biggest recommendation was to fix the product!

However, despite what engineers may desire, product performance is necessary to win, but it is often not sufficient. You need, as Dr. Moon implores, to be different (on something that matters).

The need for more than product parity was highlighted in one situation. The team was developing a service designed to compete with Dropbox, offering cloud storage and file sharing. The team, a group of engineers, was delighted when their testing indicated performance at parity with Dropbox—they felt they had succeeded in creating a competitive product. When we pointed out that parity is not competitive, especially when the competitor is established and the new entrant is not, the engineers said, "We're not worried. Dropbox has only five percent penetration; we'll win our 'fair share' of the rest since our product is just as good." Maybe, but unlikely. Dropbox is a networked product where the benefit for each user grows as the user base grows. So, while the products were the same, theirs lacked the difference of an existing user base.

In today's marketplace, networked products abound. Microsoft Office dominates because each new user benefits from the millions with whom he or she can now easily share documents, and each of the existing users benefits from having more new users to share with. The same with Facebook and LinkedIn—every added user benefits the whole user base and makes it harder for a competitor to catch up.

Make sure your product delivers the essential benefits but also make sure you are better on something that matters.

44

Insight Communities—
Faster, Cheaper, Better

We've become advocates for insight communities. It is rare that a tool can be faster, cheaper and better, but these are.

Ted Levitt teaches us to focus on the outcome (hole) and not the tool (drill). But sometimes there are tools that do a great job making just the hole we want, which is senior management engagement with useful insights into the voice of the customer.

At SingTel, we set up two insight communities (also called customer insight panels) with a company called Vision Critical (VC). Insight communities are groups of people recruited for a specific purpose, usually from among the customers of a single company, who agree to complete surveys and other tasks for that company. The company is identified, so the "sponsor" is known, and participants often, but not always, receive sweepstakes entries, prizes, or other incentives for participating. Unlike traditional research panels, all responses from insight communities are retained so you do not have to repeat questions and can target questions based on prior survey responses.

After joining SingTel, it was clear to us that many of their digital initiatives would benefit from customer analytics. However, the project leaders cited tight timelines and lack of budget as reasons for moving ahead without such insight. This is not uncommon—too much research takes too long to do and costs too much.

The insight communities addressed these obstacles and ultimately led to the various teams receiving useful, timely input—something that was very much needed because the findings often suggested that customers had a different view of what made a product desirable from that of the engineers designing the product.

How does an insight community do this?

It does require a bit of preparation and funding. In our case, we recruited 10,000 participants (we called them SingTel Digital Advisors and Optus Digital Advisors) and placed them on the VC platform. There was a fixed cost involved, but no incremental cost for any surveys. This allowed us to deliver fast findings (a week or less, sometimes in as little as a day) at no cost to the product teams.

To become faster, we also changed the process as too much time was spent designing and interpreting surveys. The relevant analogy here is buying a Ferrari: a Ferrari can drive fast but not if you use an untrained driver on crowded city streets.

To deliver speed, we instituted a process where the product team briefed us on their information needs. We then created a short survey, in Microsoft Word, in a few hours. The next day, we reviewed the survey with the product team—everyone who wanted input had to be there or had to send in comments beforehand—this eliminated endless rounds of questionnaire discussion. From the revised questionnaire, we moved in hours to the online version. The VC tool made this easy; our team would usually do the programming in an hour or so.

The following day, we did an online review of the survey—people commented on exactly what the respondent would see (which often lead to good changes). The VC tool allowed for real-time changes to the survey. One time we noticed that we were missing a "not applicable" column and watched, during the review meeting, as the missing column appeared on the screen as we spoke.

All surveys had to be 10 minutes or fewer, we did not allow the client to throw in the kitchen sink—we collaborated to focus on the few pieces of information that were really needed.

After we agreed on the changes in this second meeting, the survey was updated and launched, usually the next day (but sometimes within minutes). Results came back quickly: within 48 hours we usually had most of our responses (with 50 percent or more response rates to invitations). Then, because we had focused on the few key questions, we could easily pull down the data and provide the results to the business users.

By focusing on key questions and streamlining the process, we went from request for information to results in five to seven days. This resolved the timing and cost objections and led to the infusion of much more customer input into key decisions.

Insight communities do not work for all situations; they do not cover non-customers (as you usually recruit among customers) and they are not purely representative (so be careful on metrics that require this). However, they provide a depth of insight and customer engagement unmatched elsewhere.

For example, our surveys were short but still robust. We could add demographics to any survey, because we had them from the customers' initial profiles. Of course, we had to assume if you were a twenty-nine-year- old male last week that you were the same this week—not a very challenging assumption.

We also could easily append responses from prior surveys, so if we wanted to understand version two of a concept, we could compare it for those who liked version one and those who did not. Also, we could append product ownership from other surveys, providing more depth of insight without burdening respondents with long questionnaires.

This did not just change the product team's perspective on the voice of the customer, it changed senior management's desire to hear the customer's voice. We remember being told of one meeting where the division CEO asked for the customer reaction to the product concept. On being informed that they did not have any, the CEO said, "Then go use Mike's thing to get some." When time and cost factors were removed, the desire for customer analytics grew, and productively so.

A few anecdotes illustrate the power of insight communities to deliver on better, faster, and cheaper.

One time we tested a name for a new online dining site. A few days after the test, we received a message from one community member who wrote "I kept trying to remember the name you asked us about last week but all that kept coming to my mind was "eat sh*t." That was valuable input, as you never want your product name to remind people of sh*t, especially a dining product! But think about this, in normal research the respondent doesn't know who the sponsor is, so they can't communicate with them, and they probably wouldn't want to, they have no connection to you other than a random survey. Insight community respondents can reach you and they feel connected enough to do so.

Another time we had tested a webpage for a B2B community. One gatekeeper disliked, but couldn't find fault with, the conclusions so he attacked the research. As a B2B product, companies might have one, two or even three suppliers and he claimed that if we had looked at clients with multiple providers then the results would have been different. We hadn't asked for this information, but we could easily get it. An hour later we followed up with the original respondents and asked how many suppliers they had: one simple question. By the next morning, we had enough answers and by mid-morning we had the comparison done: no difference between those with one, two or three providers. The new website design was approved and launched!

Speed not only delivered results quickly, it allowed us to iterate quickly. We didn't allow long surveys, but clients didn't mind because if we left out an important question, we could ask it to the same people a week later.

This helped keep questionnaires short and focused.

Management agreed to cover the cost of the communities within the team budget, the business units were not charged. This removed the cost barrier to usage. We used the communities intensively, around 150 times in the first year. The cost efficiency was clear: a similar amount of activity through traditional tools would have cost five times as much at least, and we couldn't have done some of the work at all, and certainly not as fast.

We could go on about community panels, because we are real fans of them and their ability to encourage marketers and others to bring the voice of the customer into business decisions. We won't, but you can learn more if you go to our website, mikesherman.net, and look for the insight community presentation.

SECTION SIX

COMMUNICATION:
WHAT'S THE STORY, JERRY?

The next few chapters are not about analysis but rather communication. We've added them to this book because we've often observed that poor communication inhibits impact more than the quality of the findings. When we joined Synovate, we expected to spend most of our time helping teams deliver better results by helping them design and conduct more relevant and leading-edge research and analysis. But what we found was that, often, what was missing was not a good result but a good communication of that result. In the following pages, we offer our advice on how to deliver a clear, compelling communication of your actionable insights after you've done the right analysis or research.

Here we share:

- Why concise, compelling reports are needed and welcomed by clients (Chapter 45)
- The need for a brief, verbal summary of your conclusions (Chapter 46)
- Beginning your report with a concise summary (Chapter 47)
- Creating a 10-to-20-page, decision-oriented report (Chapter 48)

- Synthesizing not just summarizing your findings (Chapter 49)
- Tips for visualizing data (Chapter 50)
- Three key points that drive successful proposals (Chapter 51)
- Advice on how to improve your answers to difficult questions (Chapter 52)

45

Why Less Is More!

An insight poorly communicated is unlikely to have impact, so it is important to be as clear in your communications as in your analysis.

Is this easy? Absolutely not. As the Frenchman Blaise Pascal keenly observed in 1657, *"Je n'ai fait celle-ci plus longue que parce que je n'ai pas eu le loisir de la faire plus courte."* (I only made this letter longer because I had not the leisure to make it shorter.)

This is a common problem across the whole research industry (and elsewhere): researchers and analysts often bury their findings in 100, 300, 500 plus page documents and the findings are so well buried that they are unlikely to be discovered, much less understood.

In one case, a team presented us with an almost 100-page report and a request to identify what additional analysis they should do—because the client had rejected the report as unhelpful (being polite, as the report was awful). Upon reading the report, we realized that all the analysis had been done, and a good answer to the client's business issue had been uncovered, but it was buried (deeply!) within a very poor report. With a bit of restructuring and streamlining (the final report was 20 pages, with the rest of the charts in an appendix), the client was delighted. Did we change the analysis or the conclusion? No. Did we make it easy for the client to understand that conclusion? Yes.

This is not a hidden issue. We often assembled roundtables of Synovate clients, and this issue almost always arose spontaneously. Clients would ask why the documents were so long and turgid. The more senior the client, the more the desire to cut to the chase, as the tagline from JGE's memorable advertising exclaimed in the 1970s: "What's the story, Jerry?"[12]

---

12.   https://www.youtube.com/watch?v=wIKyB8Ufh7Q

Sharing a clear story requires four elements:

1. An elevator speech (Chapter 46)
2. A one-page executive summary (Chapter 47)
3. A 10-to-20-page document (Chapter 48)
4. Putting all the rest of the output, if it needs to be shared, in an appendix

46
The Elevator Speech

Get your conclusions out quickly and concisely. Then follow with details and explanations.

An elevator speech is a brief (30 seconds or less) summary of your answer to the client's business or marketing problem. It is called an elevator speech because it can be delivered in an elevator between the times when your client enters and when he or she exits. Just hope you have more than two floors in between!

McKinsey teaches all consultants to have a prepared elevator speech. If you find yourself with the client and he or she asks, "How is the project going?" you do not say "Fine," or "We're learning a lot," or ask about his or her favorite sports team: you deliver the elevator speech. This is done verbally, with no charts or graphics (you're in the elevator, remember).

The elevator speech leads with the answer and then provides support, briefly.

Sometimes what to say is easy. If you are testing a new product, the answer is either, "The product exceeds the agreed benchmarks," "The product failed the benchmarks but if we improve X and Y, likely it will exceed them," or "The product failed and there are no clear improvement opportunities to address." Or more bluntly, launch, fix then launch, or kill!

Other times the key issue calls for a yes or no answer, as in "Yes, you should enter market X." Sometimes, the opening line is more complicated to craft, but in all cases, it provides a clear, concise answer to the business or marketing issue.

Only then can you include the next few sentences, which give a topline explanation of why you have reached the conclusion you have.

Often, we are asked if this is too direct, if we should not first "romance" the client and draw them into the story, building to an answer. We strongly disagree; ask almost any CMO, CEO, or senior decision maker and they will tell you the same thing: start with the answer. We are addressing business issues here, not writing a mystery novel. We call reporting that ends with the answer an "Agatha Christie report." Dame Agatha would not share the answer up front—that would have ruined the drama of her stories—but we're not mystery writers so we should not be writing mysteries.

Our favorite example of an excellent elevator speech comes from an ex-colleague, Simon Duval-Kieffer. He related a story about the presentation of a new product development report, of about 100 pages, that he was preparing to present to the CMO of his client. The CMO entered the room and said he was eager to learn the conclusion, but unfortunately had been called away to an urgent meeting. He turned to Simon and said this was one of his highest priorities for the year, so, "What should I do?" Simon, who is a very capable and confident researcher, replied with a one-word elevator speech: "Launch!" The CMO thanked him for his answer and left the room. He returned 10 minutes later, because the urgent meeting had been a ruse, and he said he wanted to understand the support for Simon's conclusion. However, he explained that before enduring a one- or two-hour meeting, he wanted to make sure the team was focused on his need to make a decision. What he wanted was an elevator speech!

47

A One-Page Executive Summary

This is the first page of any report. Tell the client up front what he or she hired you to help with.

P&G, at least 30 years ago, but probably now as well, extolled the virtue of the one-page memo. Get all the key information up front. Give the answer, the key supporting facts, and the next steps. This was drummed into us by our brand managers, advertising managers, and senior management. Do not waste their time, get to the point.

The same is true of communicating insights. The first page gives the answer and the key support and, as appropriate, next steps. If the audience needs to first be reminded of the objective, fit that in too. But keep it to one page.

Here again, we are often asked if we do not first need to share the data, bring the client along on a journey, before giving the summary. Our answer: that works for Agatha Christie but not for your client. Clients do not want to spend the whole meeting wondering where all this data is leading. Give them the conclusion, then share the details.

And all on one page. Once we were parachuted into a troubled client situation in Southeast Asia. The client had been presented a 700-page report and was confused as to what it meant and, more importantly, what they should do. As we headed to the airport, we asked the team to send the executive summary, because there was no way we were going to read and digest 700 pages (and neither will any client!). So they sent it to us—all 300 pages of it. That is not an executive summary. An executive summary is one page.

Sometimes all you need is that first page. For one project in Singapore, we had introduced the Synovate team to the one-page executive summary, and the team had labored over it in detail to get it right. That meant rewriting it a dozen or more times (they were struggling with both the conclusion and how to concisely communicate it). But the experience made believers of the team (which was the head of the Hong Kong office, Jill Telford, and the head of Hong Kong qualitative, Brendan Shair, a very experienced and senior team). Why? Because they hardly got past the executive summary. The client probed and prodded them on the summary and then said, "I got it, I don't need to see the details, I trust you." What then happened was one of the best research meetings ever because the team engaged with the client (the CEO of his division) on how to revise the conclusion based on the new, critical information he proceeded to share with them. In this way, a standard presentation turned into an engaging dialogue.

The same happened at SingTel. In presenting results of some leading-edge research to the head of a division, he said, "I got it, now let's talk about how to make this happen."

48

The 10-To-20 Page Report

Clients love reports that make a clear, actionable recommendation and then support that recommendation with concise analysis.

Creating this type of report requires focusing on the information that matters and putting the rest of the material in appendices (or deleting it totally as likely it is unnecessary).

Anyone wanting to write a great report should read and digest *The Pyramid Principle* by Barbara Minto. This was the bible of reporting, taught to every consultant at McKinsey and many other professional service firms.

Concise Report Structure

20 Pages!

COVER PAGE	EXECUTIVE SUMMARY A. B. C. 1	BACKGROUND 2	
POINT A • 1 • 2 • 3 3	CHART 1 4	CHART 2 5	CHART 3 6
POINT B • 4 • 5 • 6 7	CHART 4 8	CHART 5 9	CHART 6 10
POINT C • 7 • 8 • 9 11	CHART 7 12	CHART 8 13	CHART 9 14
OTHER FINDINGS 10. 11. 12. 15	CHART 10 16	CHART 11 17	CHART 12 18
NEXT STEPS 19	APPENDIX 20		

In essence, this report contains the following:

Page 1

The executive summary, the answer, and the three (or two or four) key supporting points

Page 2

The project background, if needed (but usually not presented because this is usually known by people before they attend the meeting)

Page 3

The first supporting point, further explained

Pages 4–7

The few charts or key visuals supporting this explanation

Page 8

The second supporting point, further explained

Pages 9–11

The few charts or key visuals supporting this explanation

Page 12

The third supporting point, further explained

Pages 13–15

The few charts or key visuals supporting this explanation

Page 16

Other interesting findings (otherwise known as stuff someone insisted on including but that actually has nothing to do with the conclusion)

Page 17
Summary and next steps

For those familiar with the work of Dale Carnegie, you will recognize, from *How To Win Friends and Influence People*: Page 1: executive summary Tell them what you are going to tell them, Pages 3–15: Tell them, Page 17: summary and next steps. Tell them what you told them

Where do all the other 100 or 200 or 500 pages go? Into the circular file. Or if you really need them, into a detailed appendix. However, the appendix is just a data dump, so no effort is made to tell a story. Best to just organize the data by the questionnaire structure or discussion guide outline.

Disciplining ourselves to write a concise report is not easy. With the common data dump, there is the security that the key facts are in there, somewhere. With a concise report, the onus is on us to make sure every page is the right one; it is not 20 random pages.

When we first joined Synovate, we convinced a team to try this new approach with an interim report, which they did. The team had a very productive presentation, focused on helping the client understand a difficult market (this was an American financial services company exploring entering the Chinese market). But beforehand, the team confided that while they liked the output, this would create a lot of additional work; they were sure they would still be required by the client to do the traditional 100- to 200-page report. To their pleasant surprise, the 25 pages we presented were both well received and sufficient—the client never asked for the "full" report.

Repeatedly, we have had the reverse happen. We would work with a team to prepare a short report, only to have the research manager insist on adding in this "killer" chart or that piece of information that was sure to be requested. This often resulted in a concise report being bloated to twice the necessary size. Once this happened with a tracking report for a European client that covered mainland China, Hong Kong, and Taiwan. Fortunately, the department head was a few minutes late joining the meeting and asked, "Where are we?" We interrupted (we are not known for being shy) and said, "We're just about to go through the 45-page report, but the core findings are on just 15 pages." Her reply: "Then let's just look at the 15 pages." We did consult one or two of the other pages in response to questions, but the meeting went well, and next time the research manager accepted the shorter format (with an extensive appendix).

Sometimes you just need to see this in action to believe that less really is more.

49

A So-what About So-whats

Synthesize, Don't Summarize.

A Summary is a shortened list of something that doesn't add insight; Synthesis is the "so-what" of a list: it tells you not what something *is*, but what it *means*. When writing your headlines or conclusions, seek to synthesize, not just summarize.

In training, we use the following example:

Facts:
- I broke my knee
- A burglar knocked in my car window
- I got a speeding ticket

Summary:
My knee, car and pocketbook were all damaged recently.

Synthesis:
I've been living dangerously.

An excellent example comes from Nora Ephron, via the book *Made to Stick* by Chip and Dan Heath, who describes a lesson in writing news headlines.

Ephron still remembers the first day of her journalism class, Ephron's teacher announced the first assignment: Write the lead of a newspaper story. The teacher reeled off the facts: "Kenneth L. Peters, the principal of Beverly Hills High School, announced today that the entire high school faculty will travel to Sacramento next Thursday for a colloquium in new teaching methods. Among the speakers will be anthropologist Margaret Mead, college president Dr. Robert Maynard Hutchins, and California governor Edmund 'Pat' Brown.

According to Ephron, she and most of the other students produced leads that reordered the facts and condensed them into a single sentence: "Governor Pat Brown, Margaret Mead, and Robert Maynard Hutchins will address the Beverly Hills High School faculty Thursday in Sacramento … blah, blah, blah." The teacher collected the leads and scanned them rapidly. Then he laid them aside and paused for a moment. Finally, he said, "The lead to the story is 'There will be no school next Thursday.'"

An additional example comes from the Korean pharmaceutical research (mentioned in Chapter 29). The research objective was to assess competitive brand strength. The usual output is a table full of data, forcing the reader to search for the so-whats. But in this case the agency brilliantly summarized the findings in one chart, with no numbers. They synthesized the findings into Superior, Competitive and Follower and then used the internationally recognized stop light colors of red, yellow and green to clearly communicate the findings.

Company A Has Leading Preference In All But Pediatrics And Psychology
Share of Preference, Percent, by Specialty

					FOLLOWER	COMPETITIVE	SUPERIOR	
	ENDO	CARDIO	RESPIRA	GASTRO	Clinic IM	PED	Clinic PSY	GH PSY
CLIENT	S	S	S	S	S	C	F	F
B								
C								S
D							S	
E								
F						C		

Look for the meaning in your story so that you are synthesizing the data and not just summarizing it.

50
Data Visualization

There are good uses and bad uses of most chart forms. Certain formats are just better at telling the story, while others are awful. We mostly know the difference, intuitively, but often our output suggests otherwise.

Below, we share our thoughts on the use (and misuse) of several common chart formats. We don't pretend this is anything close to a comprehensive review of chart formats, just some helpful thoughts on very common formats.

Why use a pie chart? Hungry? Or do you want to talk about share, because a pie chart should always add up to 100 percent.

When Should You Use A Pie (or Doughnut) Chart?

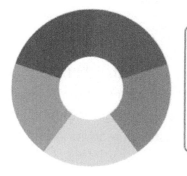

- To show a static share (i.e. 100%) distribution breakdown
- When you are hungry

We rarely encourage the use of pie charts as humans have a difficult time interpreting small differences in angles. Height—as is used in bar charts—is much easier to interpret for the human eye. However, we mention pie charts as you should be aware that they can be used to mislead (which we do not support). By angling the bottom slice of the pie chart to a user, you may make it appear larger. Steve Jobs was known for this trick, in which he would angle Apple's market share in a pie chart toward the user to make it undeservedly appear more impressive.[13]

Want to compare share between two markets? Do not use a pie chart. A side-by-side stacked bar chart is far better for conveying the comparison.

When Should You Use A Stacked Bar Chart?

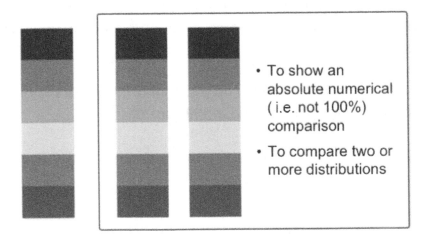

- To show an absolute numerical (i.e. not 100%) comparison
- To compare two or more distributions

Should your bar chart be vertical or horizontal? Both display the same data, but vertical images are better at conveying relative differences versus horizontal ones. But if you are comparing medical specialists use a horizontal chart because it is much easier to read long labels when they are horizontal.

---

13. https://paragraft.wordpress.com/2008/06/03/the-chart-junk-of-steve-jobs/

When Should You Use A Horizontal Bar Chart?

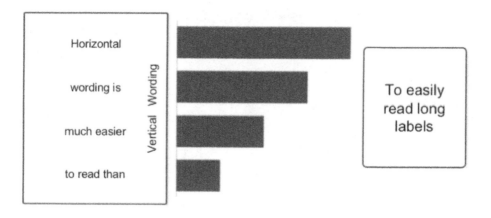

A line chart implies trend data so don't connect the dots unless you want to show a trend. When determining the size of the chart, research has shown that the human eye is best able to interpret 45-degree angles.

When Should You Use A Line Chart?

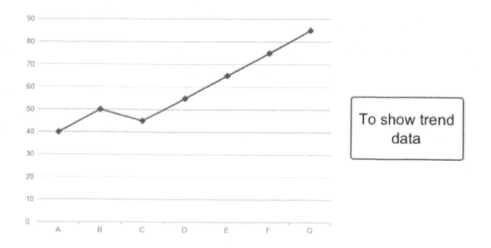

When communicating overlap, a Venn diagram is very helpful.

When Should You Use A Venn Diagram?

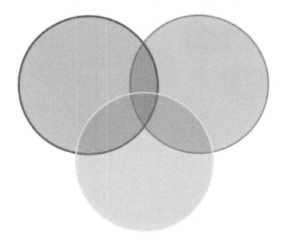

To show overlap between two or more groups

Finally, make all your charts work hard.

Start with a prescriptive title (tell me what the data means) followed by, if necessary, a descriptive subtitle (what the data is). Then place your chart key in the best spot: people read down and left to right (in most languages) so if you have a chart key, put it in the upper right-hand corner. Why? So the reader will see it before he or she confronts the data. We often see chart keys at the bottom of the chart, which means the reader sees the data, does not know what it means, and gets confused. Then the reader sees the chart key and has to look again to understand the message. Not very user friendly.

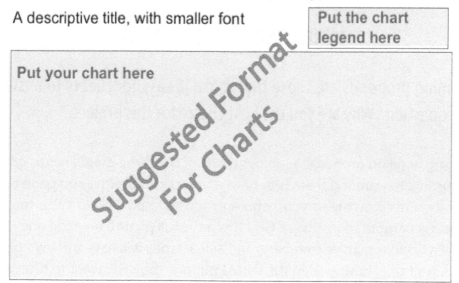

Source: should be shown in small font, as should the text of the question

We have a fun presentation that reminds us of the good and not-so-good users of many chart forms. The above are only a few examples; you can find others on our website: www.mikesherman.net/52things/charts.

51

Proposals That Sell

Winning proposals are those that make it easy for clients to answer the question "Why are you the best choice for this project?"

Writing winning proposals employs many of the same guidelines as good reporting. Key among them is to have a one-page summary on page one. Many clients won't read your whole proposal, especially if it is a turgid, 40-page or more monstrosity. Give them the full picture on page one (e.g. write a good executive summary) and at least they will have the key points (and, we hope, having seen the whole picture, they will want to dive into some of the details).

What else do winning proposals contain?

1. An explicit answer to the question "Why should you pick our firm over our competitors for this project?" Is that not ultimately the Jerry Maguire question for any proposal?
2. A rationale for why you are making the recommendations contained in the proposal. Too often, proposals focus solely on what you will do, but not why.
3. Alternatives. Nothing makes it clearer to a client why your proposal is the best than when you share credible alternatives and explain why you did not use them. This is also a great way to denigrate your competitors' proposals when you know what they will recommend and you believe you have a better answer.

Using these, and a few other, key proposal writing lessons can increase your win rate, as seen in several markets at Synovate. But applying them takes time. As with a short report, a shorter proposal takes more time to create—the fewer pages need to work harder and be more carefully crafted. So doing this means initially investing more time writing (and editing) proposals. However, once this becomes the standard, the time and resource problem solves itself, as with a higher win rate, you need to write fewer proposals to achieve the same level of sales.

One way to manage the transition is to ensure that you're investing in writing winning proposals for A and B growth situations, where the outcome matters, and if you must, sending a standard proposal to C clients. (See Chapter 42 for a discussion of account priorities.)

Writing well-crafted proposals is fundamental to winning business for many companies and yet proposals are often and long, turgid and unengaging. As with writing good reports, concisely focusing on the few things that matter rather than burdening the reader with unwanted details (which go in the appendix) can vastly improve the output and the results.

52
The Question Behind The Question

Do not just answer the question posed, but answer the question behind the question. That is, think about why the person is asking a question and what information the person is truly seeking—albeit indirectly.

The best example we have for this comes from the book *The New Leader's 100-day Action Plan* by George Bradt, Jayme Check and Jorge Pedraza. In Chapter 2, the authors make the point that in a job interview, the interviewer is always asking just three questions. Those three questions are:

1. Can you do the job?
2. Will you love the job?
3. Can I tolerate working with you?

If you are being interviewed and answering questions like: "What are your key strengths?", "How would your co-workers describe you?", "Give me examples of failures from which you learned a lesson," or our McKinsey interview favorites like: "How many pharmacies are there in Manhattan?" or "Why are manhole covers round?", do not just answer the questions. Rather, consider which of the three above is also being asked and answer in a way that addresses the question behind the question as well.

P.S. Manhole covers are round so that they won't fall in on someone who goes down the manhole. But our favorite answer is that manhole covers are round because manholes are round!

Conclusion
The Answer To The Ultimate Question Of Life, The Universe, And Everything

We didn't write this book around a grand theme, rather it is a collection of anecdotes drawn from our experience—anecdotes that we hope illustrate for the reader practical aspects of analyzing consumers and their data.

Our last anecdote is a message to readers that you (we) shouldn't let ourselves off the hook: doing the right things and doing them right matters.

In one piece of market research, we incorporated data from a national survey on risk factor behaviors (e.g. likelihood to smoke or engage in other risky behaviors). The questions were encoded, requiring a data dictionary to comprehend. In reviewing the data, it was clear that whoever had created the dictionary put little thought into how it would be used and who would use it. Definitions lacked clear delimiters, names randomly extended across multiple lines, and some definitions were missing entirely. Lack of care meant the 100 plus-page questionnaire required manual encoding. This lack of care for the details likely occurred because the data collector didn't analyze the data themselves. One common thread of our book is that without useful data we lack the means to create useful outputs. We hope that our stories will encourage you to consider what data is useful and how it will be used.

Here are the six key takeaways we hope you get from this book:

1. Show them the money
2. Pick the right metrics
3. Think about what data you should collect, don't boil the ocean
4. Understand your data before beginning to analyze it
5. Use good drills to create the right holes
6. Communicate clearly and concisely

Overall, we hope this book helps you to ask the right questions. It would be a shame to wait seven-and-a-half million years to find the answer is 42 before realizing that you do not know the question that it answers.[14]

---

14. Source: Video of 42   https://www.youtube.com/watch?v=sgeMrzbfrxg

Acknowledgements

Our thanks for many years of collaboration, guidance, and mentoring that was instrumental in the lessons shared in this book.

Mike:

I'd like to thank, in alphabetical order, Dave Acorn, Jim Bemowski, Adrian Chedore, Bob Dennis, Cuong Do, Chuck Farr, Melissa Gil, Josh Goff, John Forsyth, George Haylett, Jannie Hofmyer, Scott Lee, Giuseppe Manai, Tim McGuire, Victoria Nam, Andrew Parsons, Martin Roll, Stuart Romm, Dean Rubin, John Sallay, Amy Shi-Nash, Mark Singer, Jill Telford and Kurt Thompson. I'm sure there are others who should be listed here and are not, please put this down to my poor memory and not my lack of appreciation for what you taught me.

But most of all, I'd like to acknowledge my collaborator in this effort, my son Alex Sherman. This book came out of many conversations he and I had about customer analytics—if not for his pushing me to capture and share that material, this book would not exist.

Alex:

I'd like to thank, in alphabetical order, Karthik Balakrishnan, Mike Cangi, Charles Chiang, Brett Fisher, Kevin Footer, David Hardoon, Prabhu Kapaleeswaran, Mahmoud Lababidi, Kimberly Link, Brian Linton, Kevin Markham, Audrey Mars, Aleks Ontman, Anthony Seeton, Rob Smith, Stephen Wolff, Jun Yao and Rob Yoegel.

Mike and Alex:

We'd like to also thank those who specifically helped us with this book. We take full responsibility for all grammatical errors and poorly written phrases and thank those who helped us minimalize both: Sharon Cooper, Debra Weiss Geline and Rachel Wilson.

About The Authors

Mike Sherman
Marketing, Customer Insight, and CRM/Big Data Expert

Mike has almost 30 years of marketing, market research, and CRM/Big Data experience. He helps companies address marketing opportunities through understanding end users' needs, turning those needs into insight/data specifications, and converting that output into clear, actionable results.

Mike began his career at Procter & Gamble, where he managed both new and established brands. He spent 17 years with McKinsey & Company; while there he created their Asia-Pacific marketing practice and was a founder of their global CRM practice. Mike was also Global Head of Knowledge Management for Synovate, where he lead efforts to improve the value clients obtain from research. At SingTel and Hong Kong Telecom he drove the use of both customer data and customer research to help the business understand customer and customer data opportunities.

Based in Asia since 1997, Mike has worked across the region and has extensive experience in the FMCG, retail, financial services, and telecoms industries.

Mike holds an MBA, high distinction (Baker Scholar), from Harvard Business School and two bachelor's degrees, magna cum laude, from the Wharton School and College, University of Pennsylvania.
He frequently speaks on marketing, big data and customer insights at conferences and has been published several times in the McKinsey Quarterly on marketing issues in developing and Asian markets. He is

also the former board chair of AFS-USA, a leading high school foreign exchange organization, and an avid traveler, having visited more than 125 countries.

A full list of Mike's articles, speeches, and press mentions is available at www.MikeSherman.net

•••

Alex Sherman
Data Scientist, Customer Analytics Enthusiast

Alex helps companies manage big data challenges by applying machine learning and natural language processing technologies.

Alex works as a data scientist practitioner and instructor at a leading global technology firm, specializing in the design and implementation of informatics and analytics software development projects. Previously, he interned with the analytics software vendor SAS in Singapore, two Philadelphia based start-ups, Monetate and United By Blue, and a not for profit in New York, AFS Intercultural Programs.

Alex is passionate about teaching the practical application of machine learning. He is a lead instructor for General Assembly where he teaches a 10-week data science bootcamp. His instructor bio is available at the following URL: https://generalassemb.ly/instructors/alex-sherman/6897.

Alex has lived, worked, and studied across the globe in the United States, South Africa, Hong Kong, and Singapore. He has a bachelor of business administration, summa cum laude, from Temple University and is studying at the University of Pennsylvania for a Master of Computer and Information Technology.

Made in the USA
Coppell, TX
12 January 2021